The Bottom is Six Feet Under

VALERIE COVERT

authorHOUSE®

AuthorHouse™
1663 Liberty Drive
Bloomington, IN 47403
www.authorhouse.com
Phone: 1-800-839-8640

PHOTO CREDIT: *Matthew's Head Stone by Valerie Covert*

© 2010 Valerie Covert. All rights reserved.

No part of this book may be reproduced, stored in a retrieval system, or transmitted by any means without the written permission of the author.

First published by AuthorHouse   3/8/2010

ISBN: 978-1-4490-8463-9 (e)
ISBN: 978-1-4490-8461-5 (sc)
ISBN: 978-1-4490-8462-2 (hc)

Library of Congress Control Number: 2010923916

Printed in the United States of America
Bloomington, Indiana

This book is printed on acid-free paper.

This book is dedicated to many people.

**Firstly to our daughter who is the brightest light and…
the gift from God that taught us both unconditional love…..
and who remains my inspiration for each and every day.**

Secondly to those who are struggling with drug addiction (or any substance addiction) and those who their addiction affects.

To Matthew's family and his "true" friends (not many of which are mentioned in his diary).

Acknowledgements

I would like to thank the following people for helping me to bring this book to completion, for seeing it in me:

To my friend, Dr. Tina Thomas (this NEVER would have happened without her encouragement and without me "owing" her one), my mother, who gave me the encouragement daily to see this to completion, (by saying "You need to finish that book of yours!"), my friend Ann (Matthew's ex-girlfriend) who inspired me to not stop when the emotions seemed to be too hard and who proof read it for me and insisted that I finish it, to Matthew's cousin Dana (quite possibly one of his most favorite people in his world)... and definitely one of the most favorite people in my world. She is the one who came to my side and helped me through the entire process that was awaiting me and helping me all the way, to the man in my life now, Jasen for supporting me through the whole process...who tries his very best to take a position of some form of "fatherhood" for my daughter.

Lastly to Matt, for leaving me his story to be told.

Preface

Dear Reader,

 To be totally honest, I have created this book as a sort of therapy for myself. Just to get it out there. That's not the only reason of course. I have also created it in the hope that it will reach someone who is struggling and they will not only READ but also FEEL the insanity that is drug addiction. Maybe make a change.

 The pages in Matt's diary are 100% genuine and are straight from the diaries that Matthew kept. I have only omitted a few things that I believe would be hurtful to people. I've kept the most of the spelling the same, not to show ignorance, Matthew was not an ignorant man, but to show the depth of the insane effect that certain substances have on your brain. I feel that it is important to honestly depict what he was going through. Some of it was written when he was very high or "coming down" and is what some will consider incoherent babble. Some was written when he would be sober ... trust me; you will be able to tell the difference.

 I have made very few grammatical and punctuation corrections. I have arranged the dates and times the best I could. The actual writings (that you will see in the copied pages) were run together and hard to decipher. The spelling you will read is how he spelled the words. There is even an instance where he writes the wrong year. You can see at the end of this book a few copies of actual pages from his journal to show that I am not embellishing anything and so that you can see some of the pictures drawn where I say (drawn happy face, etc.)

 Although Matt would probably at times have thought that we didn't understand him and that we were "against" him, we all loved him deeply.

Valerie Covert

Matthew's addiction was a struggle for all of us as well, but at the heart, our love never wavered. We still miss him every day. This is a very personal story in small part about us but in large part about addiction.

I thought I knew Matt very well. Even after our split, we remained very close and spoke almost every day, but I was shocked at some of the things that I read in his journals. When I received them, I sat down on the floor and read them both cover to cover.

The people he mentions, or the parts these people play (most of which I don't know personally – a few he had spoken about) - are as follows. I did not change the names. There are no last names used. Anonymity, right?

> Chip = His dealer.
>
> Lance = A friend of Chip.
>
> Billy & Ashley = dealers.
>
> Jessica = his daughter.
>
> Valerie/Val = me. His ex-wife and forever friend.
>
> Sue – A good friend who gave Marissa to him and helped him to care for her.
>
> Teri – A friend.
>
> Lisa – A girl that he was renting a room from
>
> Karrie – An old friend of his and mine (she and I parted ways in about 1994)
>
> Turtle – Karrie's son – my former God Son.
>
> Dave – A friend with Matt at the end of his life. There is a picture of the two of them dated 11/23/02 in his last journal.
>
> Marissa – His pet iguana.
>
> Janis – An ex-girlfriend.
>
> Henry The Boy – his lifelong childhood friend that he grew up with and carried the utmost respect for until the end of his days.

Henry the Dog

All of the others I never knew about.

Definition of some words used:

Ish / issue (the drugs in the needle)

The Bottom is Six Feet Under

Rig – The needle

BG – Blood Glucose – for the "normal" diabetic ranges should be between 80 and 120. - Please keep that in mind as he enters his blood glucose level a lot in the journal. After so many years of drug abuse and not treating his diabetes correctly, his body functioned at very high levels. Levels that would have been lethal to other diabetics. Many times we went to the emergency room when he would get sick and the nurses would take his blood sugar and immediately jump into a fury of trying to get him regulated.

"r" – regular insulin

"n" – novilin

"h" – humulin (pre-mixed)

Matt's drug of choice was crystal meth. Because he was a diabetic, he always had access to needles so he didn't snort it…of course; it started out that way, but soon switched to injecting it. What they call "slamming" it. After a while, he was drawn to people who did the drug the same way. We were never rich. We were barely getting by paycheck to paycheck. But, Matt rarely had to pay money for his drugs. He would trade his needles for free dope. In the rare occasion that he had to have money, he would take our household possessions (as well as Jessica's movies and toys) and sell them at the local swap meets.

Matthew had a few true friends in his life. There was Henry the boy… (as opposed to Henry the dog – Matthew's childhood dog) and TJ. And myself. The three of us, no matter how frustrated we got or how much tough love we had to use, we were steadfast friends to Matt. I met Matt through TJ. Ironically enough, when I was pregnant with Jessica, TJ's girlfriend at the time was also pregnant. They had a son born one month after Jess. Today, April 9, 2007, as I am writing this, I am in shock. I got in touch with TJ just today. He told me that the mother of his son, just a few years ago, passed away from drug abuse. And of course, there is Matthew's family. They too were frustrated, angry and confused but remained true to Matt. I'd like to take a moment to let you know about Matthew's family. All of whom I hold very dear. His father was one of the most incredible men that I have ever known. Mind you, he had an alcohol problem to beat any you've ever hear of, but yet still, to me, was an incredible man. He had, and taught to his sons, a respect for women that is unheard of anymore. He comes from the old days. He was a hard ass. A REAL hard ass. Especially to Matt. In no way do I want to disrespect his memory, but I do believe that he was a HUGE part of Matt's social, mental, physical, etc. problems. There was a time Matt would talk about (not in too much detail) when his father was so drunk and had taken so many pain pills that he tried to stuff Matt into the clothes dryer. Mind you, Matt was about 12 or 13 years old. There was a time when his father suffered a major on the job injury and cut of two and a half of his fingers. The doctors prescribed him many different pain medications and along with the alcohol…, Matt's problems at home were just getting worse. His father made him stay home from school so he could take care of him. His father drank, took huge amounts of pills, and counted on Matt to take care of his every drunken, drug induced need. And he wasn't nice about it.

He also rarely called him Matt. For some reason, he had decided to call him or bellow to him "Mack". I never really understood that. But I can still hear it in my head. Henry (who has now grown out of the title of Henry the Boy and is now know as Hank), still refers to him with that name.

In spite of all of the abuse (and, something that I've come to learn is very common) Matthew stood true to his father and loved him with all his heart. As did I. For years after we were married we would go to his father and step-mother's house every Friday night for pizza.

His father cared deeply for me and treated me as his daughter. I suspect he was also hoping that there was some way that I could help Matt. We all thought love could help.

After we found out we were pregnant, I remember his dad being ecstatic at the idea of Matt having to "grow up" and be a dad…and for himself being a grandpa. I remember once, when Jess was about 3 months old, his dad looked at me and said, "You look beautiful." I said "Thank you." And he replied, "No, I mean you look so wonderful. Motherhood really agrees with you. You look so happy."

His mother and I were very close. She was also ecstatic at the prospect of becoming a grandmother. She loved Matt dearly and I suspect that she loved me or at least loved the idea that maybe being with me and a baby, he would stop doing drugs. Matt's mother took the role of my mother for a time and to this day, I hold her close to my heart. She is married to a wonderful man who has and had stood by her and supported her with his whole heart. He loved Matt too. He was as frustrated as the rest of us.

You know, they always say in rehabs that the only 3 results of drug abuse are Jails, Institutions and Death. Do addicts not really believe this? Matt has done time in jail. Matt has been hospitalized and in rehabs. Matt died.

I believe that drug abuse by one single person is like a fungus, but the addict doesn't realize how far it spreads. They think that they are only hurting themselves...their bodies...it's nobody else's business. They say that you try and get help once you have hit "rock bottom". I believe that the bottom is six feet under.

I will try and not make this about our story too much. But I believe that a little background is necessary for you to understand a little about who Matt was and the kind of man he was. I want this to remain Matt's story. I want the focus to be on his journal entries and the craziness of the drug abuse.

Whether and addict or the family or friend of an addict, I ask only one thing of you as you read this, please do so with an open mind and without judgment. We are all human.

With Warmest Regards,
Valerie Covert

Introduction

My purpose for writing this book, as I've stated before, is a form of therapy for myself. Mostly it is for an addict. Any addict. If you are currently in rehabilitation center reading this, first, congratulations and good luck. There are people out there pulling for you. Even people you don't personally know. I am pulling for you. Secondly, please read and re-read his journal entries. You know EXACTLY how he felt. I suspect that some of you may understand some of his entries better than others. You have a chance, AND there IS hope. This is an incredible chance for you to see (without living it) how un-manageable life is on drugs. There really is no other choice.

If this book can touch even one soul...one who is addicted or one who loves someone who is addicted...and gives the them any kind of comfort or understanding, I have done what I intended with this book.

You will hear how he feels from his own words and you will *feel* the progression of the sickness and the impending doom.

This is the background I mentioned earlier.

I can never claim to be innocent in all of this because for our entire history together I enabled him to do all of the things he did in one way or another because I loved him very much. I never knew a better way then to help. None of us did...we all loved...we all yelled...we all cried....we all tried to reason...we all offered anything he wanted.... He didn't even know what could help. No matter how many 12 step books he read, no matter how many meetings, no matter how many rehabs...he couldn't stop. You will see from his diary entries how he struggled all the time to stop. He would literally hide in his apartment when the dealer would come to the door (he mentions his dealer would show up with a bag of groceries and a bag of dope…you'll read that in his own words) that guy was well aware of Matt's diabetes. Apparently as you will see in his writings, drugs weren't the only illegal things that the two shared. His entries are heartbreaking as you read his struggle…"please God…don't let me answer the door…please take this feeling from me."

OUR STORY

I met Matthew when I was 13 years old. He was 17. His good friend (TJ) was dating my sister and Matt and I struck up a friendship. In fact, we were kind of instantly friends. He had a lowered red Datsun pick up truck that was the love of his life. I still have a picture of that truck. He would come and pick me up and we would go "hang out". We weren't romantic at the time. We became best friends. Eventually he began dating one of my girlfriends and the two of them together with me and my high-school boyfriend began a four-some. We were inseparable. (I still have a picture of the four of us sitting on him mother's couch when we were all hanging out.) We would always hang out together and double date. I remember the first time that we did crank. Well, for me anyway it was the first time. He had done it before. I think that it INSTANTLY had its grip on him. By the time I turned 18 (he was 21) we had departed from the other two of the four-some and I had developed a serious crush on him. We began to date. We were still in the "party mode" of life and were enjoying it.

In our partying days, he was known, at first, as the guy who would get tweaked and never shut up. At first, it was a social thing and he enjoyed doing it with other people, after a while he became a loner and would do his drugs by himself. He would stay inside and stay awake for days at a time, tweaking, carving his initials on EVERYTHING he owned. (Some of his belongings that I still have bear the scars of the carvings.) Funny, they used to make me mad. Now I take comfort in them and they make me smile because they were Matt, completely and totally Matt.

He had had a serious relationship with someone (as serious as it can be for teenagers) that had ended just before I turned 18 at the same time that my mother had progressed in her relationship that she told me she was putting the house up for sale and moving to his house. She agreed to help me get into an apartment and I knew that it was my chance to have Matt closer to me. He was in need of getting out of his parents house. He agreed to become "roommates" with me and that's where it really began…

He moved in with me. Although we didn't share a bedroom, we were intimate and getting closer every day but his drug use was out of control. He knew it and decided (along with the help of his parents) to admit himself into a 30 day in-house rehab. I was so hopeful because I knew that if he could get better, we could have a wonderful life together. He was my very best friend. We laughed and cried together. We went every where together. We knew what the other was thinking and feeling with out words being spoken. He wanted to get better. He was hopeful. We all were. He entered the rehab with every intention of NEVER doing drugs again. I would make the 2 hour drive up for the 5 hour visitation each Saturday. My heart would race at the thought of seeing him sober and so happy and feeling so well. After the 30 day program he came home. He gave me the "clues" to look for with someone doing drugs (something that would end up biting him in the end.) Things were going well. We started sharing the same bedroom and I soon became pregnant. We were both ecstatic! He got a job as a high rise window washer and I had a good job at a large insurance company. We were ready for a great life. I remember we told his parents on one of their birthdays that we were pregnant. They were not immediately thrilled about it but warmed up to the thought quickly when they saw that our intentions were to be the best parents we could be. 17 days later I had a miscarriage. I was a mess. Matt was strong, but heartbroken. He had a short relapse. I was oblivious to the re occurring problem because I was lost in my own heartbreak and misery. He came to me and said he had relapsed and wanted to get clean and start going to meetings again and re-establish contact with his sponsor. He did all of that and soon I became pregnant again. We decided to get married. His mother and I immediately started planning our wedding.

Chapter 1 (Our Story)

YEAR ONE 1991-1992

We were married on December 28, 1991. Three days after Christmas. Needless to say, Christmas was virtually ignored that year with wedding and baby plans in the works. Jessica was due to be born on June 1st. The beginning of the pregnancy was fun. We were living in a small one bedroom apartment in downtown Sacramento that I think we paid right around $400 a month for. I had a job working for a well know insurance company and Matthew was working as a high rise window washer. I guess he kind of always liked to live dangerously…if he couldn't do the drugs, and at the beginning of our marriage he was sober, he would have to do something dangerous. High Rise window cleaning for God's sake. One day while I was at work (on the 6th floor) I saw my husband dangling from two ropes and sitting on a small piece of wood with a bucket and a squeegee washing the windows of my office. Uugh! Other than his occupation, life was good. By the time I had reached my fifth month, I began to a have a few minor complications that forced me to go on disability until after the baby was born. That was a REALLY wonderful time for us. I was able to be at home every day and was nesting. I made his lunch for him to take to work everyday and there was a hot dinner on the table every night. He and I both enjoyed it. Even though he was happy with our life, he made the decision to do crank again. Soon admitted it to me, begged forgiveness, promised not to do it again…you know…all those words that the addict as well as the person who loves them believe as the truth. I started to go to meetings with him for support.

I can pretty vividly remember almost every moment of our time together. He was my very best friend. We liked to do the same things for the most part. The only thing that we didn't share was the love of the drug.

I remember the night that my water broke. He and I had come home from dinner with one set of our parents and I was exhausted. I kissed him and headed off for bed while he watched the news. I was in bed and went to roll over when I felt and heard (thought I heard anyway) a strange pop and then I jumped out of bed. I remember running to the entryway and not really screaming, but telling him loudly that my water had broken. I'll never forget the look of pure and utter fear on his face. His words were calming and his actions were accurate, but he was freaking out on the inside. It makes me smile to remember that face. We made it to the hospital with plenty of time to spare. It was 11pm when we arrived and she wasn't born until 12:37pm the next afternoon. He was a trooper. He laid on a small cot next to my bed and tried to get some sleep. With the contractions at about 10 minutes apart and me grabbing him or shaking him violently with each one, sleep was fleeting. I remember that he was wearing a yellow Nestle Quick T shirt and at one point when the contractions were particularly strong, I grabbed that t shirt and pulled him close to me and said in a voice that to this day I don't believe was my own but more like the anti Christ..."MAKE IT STOP"... He looked at me and just started to cry. He told me that if he could, he would do anything to make it stop or do it for me, but he couldn't so he would just be there and love me. I tell a funny little story about him. He used to tease me when we were pregnant and discussing baby names and he would come up with some outlandish things. Pla-sen-thia was his favorite. He had learned about placenta in Lamaze class. What a kook. He would say that he wanted to keep the placenta for reasons that I won't mention because I don't want to offend anyone and I know that some people do keep theirs and plant it or something, but we weren't like that. I kept telling him that he was sick and that there was no way that he was even going to want to know anything about it. He swore he was all about it. The funny part is that when the time came, the doctor asked him (after she had set it in a pan beside my bed and weighed it) if he would like to see it. NO ONE, has ever answered someone so quickly…"OH OH NO NO THANKS…PLEASE…NO." His face was whiter than rice. That face too makes me smile.

When Jessica was born, I didn't think that he would ever be happier and I (once again) didn't think that he would ever do crank again. The day that she was born he left the hospital for a little while and went out and got two tattoos one of her full name and birth date and the other was M+V above her name. There was never a prouder father in the world. He had every intention of being the best father that he could be.

When Matt had come home previously from rehab, he had (again) no intentions of ever doing drugs again. He explained to me in detail exactly how he would prepare the dope in a spoon (the missing spoons were quite puzzling to me, but like I said, I was oblivious as to how it was done…I can even remember asking him if he had any idea where the spoons were going. Of course he said no.) Anyway, he told me that one sure way to know if he was doing drugs again would be if I saw blood in any of his needles. It was common for us to have needles in the house with him being diabetic. "When you are a diabetic", he said to me, "you only inject medicine into your body. There is no need to draw blood. In order to shoot drugs, you have to draw a little blood first to know that you have hit a vein." He really had no intention of ever doing it again. I'm sure that he never would have given up the "clues" if he had.

When Jessica was three months old, I was walking out of the bathroom when I happened to notice a needle in the rubbish can. Something very normal in the house of a diabetic, but it struck me immediately because there was a small amount of blood in it. Oh God! My heart sank. I grabbed it out of the rubbish can and took it into the kitchen where he was. He was standing with his back to the kitchen sink, the inside of his arms clearly visible…(although I never though to check his arms). My hands shaking (as well as my voice) as I held it up for him to see. When he saw what I had, he immediately folded his arms in front of himself. I screamed at him "What is this?" What could he say. There was no getting out of it. There was no denying it. He just looked at me and started to cry.

By this time, we had only been married 9 months and there was no way I was going to give up. Although, to be honest, a part of me knew then that Jessica deserved sober parents. I wondered how we would end up. He swore that he would never do it again. Started going to meetings and separated himself from the people who did drugs. For a while.

Valerie Covert

We had an agreement when we found out that we were pregnant that I would stay at home for the first five years of Jessica's life. By the time she was 9 months old (and Matt was doing drugs again), I knew that that wasn't going to happen and that I needed to go to work and support our family. I wasn't happy and started to resent him for what I saw as taking my time away from my daughter. The worst part was that once I started working, he was more than happy to be a stay at home dad. He was even sober. From drugs anyway. He started to drink. Just about a six-pack a day. (NOT good for a diabetic).

Still, I was determined to make our family work. He was again dedicated to sobriety. We had a happy first few years.

Year Two 1992-1993

Our second year went quickly. Jessica was turning 1 and we started planning her birthday party. (Matt was a very involved father)...in fact, I remember that he was upset that he wasn't given a Baby Shower of his own. I was still as happy and hopeful as I could be and so was Matt. He loved being a daddy. I was working a full time job and learning what it really meant to have a baby. Matt was trying to stay sober. It wasn't working.

We were still in love and trying to figure things out.

Year Three 1993 – 1994

I knew that it was going to take much more than my love, or the love that he had for Jess and I to keep him from going back to the drugs again. I was at the end of my rope and didn't know what to do. I was working full-time and Matthew wouldn't get a job. I would come home at the end of the day and the baby would be walking around the house in nothing but a diaper and the house would be a mess and he would be sitting on the sofa, drinking beer and watching TV. Please know that he never neglected Jessica. She was fed and clean, just not dressed. I knew that something had to change. I was more than willing to care for my daughter, but I had real apprehensions about supporting a grown man who was capable of working but just wouldn't. I was greatly embarrassed when money was tight and his solution was to go to his parents house and empty their

The Bottom is Six Feet Under

cupboards and fridge. He used to call it "The Parent Shopping Network". His parents constantly had to help us with formula and diapers because only one job doesn't spread far. I was so disappointed. We had dreams. We were supposed to be building a life. Days were ticking by and nothing was changing. I spoke with my Mom and out of the blue she said to me…."if you leave by the end of this week, I will buy tickets for you and Jessica to go to New York and live with your sister" (my sister had a home with an attached apartment). That was one of the hardest decisions that I ever had to make. I told Matt that I didn't want to leave him, but I couldn't go on living that way, nor could he so he decided that that would be his best way to get sober (change of address…ha…another "escape"). After an EXTREMELY emotional dinner with his mother and her husband and a hearty "good luck and do this right" from his father and wife and my mother and her husband…Jess and I were on a plane that Friday. The plan was for Matt to stay and sell as much of our belongings that he could (staying clean all the while) and then to get into our little Toyota Tercel and drive from Sacramento to New York. I knew when Jess and I got onto that first plane that the chances of him being able to do this without doing drugs was going to be a HUGE test for him. Secretly, in my own head, I was testing him too. I just knew that the threat of loosing us would keep him sober. At least I hoped. So Jess and I tearfully got on the plane. In my mind it was his last chance to show me that he could handle "real life". He needed to take care of having the phone turned off, dealing with the security deposit at our apartment, all of the moving arrangements. Selling some of our things and deciding what he should keep and pack and carry in the car with him and NOT using the money for dope was the biggest test.

So I went to New York and got a job and waited. We spoke on the phone every night and he would tell me what he had gotten done. He swore he was sober. I knew better, just by the sound of his voice. My heart was broken. All I wanted was Matt back, functioning and being the husband and father that we both dreamed he'd be. I remember telling him that if he showed up strung out, there was no way that he could live with us and would need to find his own place to live. That was one of the hardest things that I ever had to say to him because I knew he was strung out, but still, I was still hopeful that he was being honest. When he showed up at my sisters Jess and I were both overjoyed to see that car pull up. Jessica's joy never ceased. As soon as I ran out the door and saw the state he was in, I knew. I knew he had sold everything and used all of the money to buy dope to cope with all he had to do…including the drive across the country. His face was so sunk in, he looked half dead. His eyes were crazy and he started telling me about seeing signs all the way (road signs) that were really signs talking to him. Then he went inside and slept for 3 days straight. I was mortified, embarrassed (I had told everyone of his arrival and mind you, my entire extended family, (aunts, uncles cousins, etc) all lived there and were anxious to meet him). Here I was making immediate excuses for his sleep. Once he finally woke up, I stood my ground and told him that he would have to find some where else to live. That broke my heart. Here we were, in a place that he had never been, and I was telling him that he couldn't be with us. I still wanted to help. He got a horrible little room at a local hotel and a night job working at the College as a janitor so he could be with Jess while I worked during the day. I spent my nights crying myself to sleep. Finally, it started to work out well. We were in a place where at least for him, at that time, it was impossible for him to find dope. He finally was sober. He was acting responsibly and trying to mend our relationship. It was actually nice to have him there with us. It was nice to have him back. I can remember starting too really "like" him again. I had never stopped loving him, but at times he was hard to like. Without the dope, he was the old Matt again. We were starting to really enjoy time together and exploring our new environment. I don't know if you've ever seen the colors change in the fall on the east coast, but it is amazing. Those colors can rejuvenate a soul and fills you with a beautiful feeling. I remember taking a drive one day, just the three of us, and how exhilarated and excited Matt was at the prospect of a sober life. We started to spend a lot of time together. He had moved out of the hotel and was rooming with a good friend of my sisters so that had allieved a lot of my guilt (I knew he wasn't alone anymore in that dingy little hole in the wall hotel room).

We got a call one day that his father and step-mother were going to come out and visit. We couldn't wait to show them our new "digs" as his dad would say. They came for about a week. We showed them around and they told us that Matt's dad was sick. He had cancer. I knew that they had come out to see us and make sure we were okay. His dad knew that it would be the last time he would see us. I have pictures of that last visit. That was in June and RD Covert passed away in August of that year. We were both very torn up by his death. Matt, incredibly, stayed sober. By April of the next year, we had decided that we needed to go back to California and live there for many reasons, New York was too cold in the winter, we were West Coast people, and our parents missed us. Matt's mother was broken hearted like you would not believe and that hurt us both badly as neither of us ever wanted to hurt her. I got my income tax return and we rented a Ryder truck, filled it with all of the things that we had accumulated in our year there and hooked up the little Toyota to the back and headed back across country on April 1st. We had a wonderful trip. Even though I was still being very stubborn and every night when we would stop at a hotel, I would insist on 2 beds, I will admit that once again, I was hopeful that we would work things out and be a family again. I have pictures of the "Welcome To" each state that we drove through. It took us about 7 days to reach Sacramento and by the time we arrived, we were exhausted. We were staying at Matt's moms house. She was thrilled to have Jessica back. I started looking for a job and planning to move into my own place ASAP. Don't get me wrong, I love Matt's mom, but living with your mother-in-law when you're in the process of leaving and possibly divorcing her son, is not an easy thing to do.

I did get a job and moved into a small apartment with Jessica and Matt started to do drugs again. I will admit to not fully understanding an addict. The entire time I kept thinking, "If he loves us enough, he will stop." In reality, he loved us more than anything, but he was "powerless" to the grip of the dope. I held out for three years before I started divorce proceedings with a broken heart and feeling completely defeated. Matt had visitation with Jess and EVERY time I would worry my self sick until she returned to me. He tried to keep a decent residence and he tried to be sober for the visits. If he wasn't…of course, I wouldn't leave here there. I can remember on one of his scheduled visits, he called me at work crying and saying that he didn't have any food to feed Jess, no money, and he couldn't take care of her. I told him to stay right there and I would come and get her. I left work and by the time I got to his place they were gone. My heart sank. He sounded so bad on the phone; I had no idea what he was doing. I called the police. I needed to find Jessica right away. The police came and took all the information and started to look for him. I found him at his mothers about an hour later. I knew then that his visitations had to be supervised from that point on.

We went on with our lives and tried to share Jessica. I eventually met a man and we decided to move to Hawaii. I saw it as a fresh start for Jess and

Valerie Covert

I. It was absolutely heartbreaking for Matt for us to move so far away. We were officially divorced in November 1997. We spoke on the phone every other day and remained close. I knew he was doing dope, but until I read the diaries, I had no idea of the extent of the chaos in his life.

I remember the morning that I got the phone call from his brother. I was excited when I saw his name on my caller ID and was ready for a pleasant, catch-up conversation. He asked me where Jess was and told him she was at school. I'll never forget his words. "Hey Valerie, how are you?" "I'm good, how are you?" I responded. "Is Jessica home?" he asked. "No", I replied, "she's at school". "I'm calling to let you know that Matt has passed away. They found him in his room." All I can remember from that point is saying…NO NO NO NO. He apologized and promised to call me with further news. I completely fell apart. The only thing that I knew is that I needed to be in California. Near him. Or near where he was. My mom booked a trip for us and made all of the arrangements. I had no idea how I was going to tell Jessica. I remember that I went to her school to pick her up and I knew that I was in no shape to tell her alone. I went and talked to the school counselor and we called her to the office. She new the moment that she saw me that something was wrong. I sat her down and told her that her daddy had died. She bawled. Quietly. We drove home both crying. There has never been anything harder in my life that I've had to do than tell my little 10 year old that the man that she believes hangs the moon is gone. I've never had to deal with a death before. I had no idea what it entailed. Apparently, because he had never re-married and I had his child, by law, I was responsible for his belongings and his parents were responsible for his remains. Through the help of my mom (I was completely numb…when I wasn't crying that is) we went the room he was renting and gathered up all of his things. I asked his family if there were any things they wanted. I spent a few days sorting through his few things and picking out items that were significant to me. Some t-shirts that smelled like him. I still keep them in zip-lock bags to retain the smell. (There was one night Jess said to me that she missed the way he smelled and I was able to run down the hall and get one of the shirts and let her smell it.) I'm glad I kept them. I kept some slippers, and old can of chew (I love the way it smells in the can), other odds and ends. I donated his car to the Kidney foundation. I had found a few pawn tickets in his things and went and paid those to make sure we could have that stuff too. I let Jess pick out anything she wanted.

The Bottom is Six Feet Under

Those are the physical things that we have left of Matt. We have pictures, we have memories. We don't have Matt.

I remember going to the morgue to see him. Jess didn't go in with me. My dad and Matt's favorite cousin Dana went with me (each holding me by the arm). It was the worst thing I've ever seen. It was really him. It looked just like him. He even had a 5 o'clock shadow. Only he was gone. My heart broke a little more.

I thought I had been falling apart the whole time, but when we got on the plane to come back to Hawaii, I really lost it. I really felt the loss then. I was leaving him there in California. I tried to stay strong for our daughter but I kept excusing myself and literally running to the rest room sobbing and trying to get a hold of myself. People on the plane watched me with sad, confused looks on their faces, wondering why I kept running down the isle toward the bathroom.

Jessica has had her own struggles with the loss of course. She suffers from the same depression that her dad did. I carry a good amount of guilt for her suffering. As I said before, I fell apart. She was only 10. She was watching her mommy barely functioning and I believe that she thought she needed to be strong for me. She told me once that she thought she was "dead" inside because she never cried too much about her dad. Only when I told her. As a teenager, she has suffered some more losses in her life and the most recent sent her into a deep depression and she came to me and told me that she wanted to die. She has had two separate instances where she has tried to commit suicide. I immediately got help for her. She was in the hospital for a short time but we won't get into all of that. That's another book in itself. I decided along with her psychiatrist that it would be good idea for her to go and visit his grave site. We did that in December (2007) and you will see at the end of this book what was written (with her permission) in the note that she left along with some flowers for him.

We are still taking things one day at a time.

In the 20 years that I knew Matt, I never knew him (or considered him) to be very religious. Once I started reading his journals I was shocked to learn how truly spiritual he was. He begs Jesus to take the agony from him, both from the drug addiction and the physical ailments that he was plagued with. He was in constant pain, the kind hopefully none of you reading this will ever have to endure. As you will read, in his words, it was torturous.

Valerie Covert

I have one journal that begins in February 2002 and the last entry is on January 22nd 2003. It basically chronicles the last year of his life. He passed away on January 29, 2003. He did not write consistently every day and the entire month of September is missing. At one point, as I mentioned, he even writes the wrong year. Please understand that some of the entries are illegible and highly drug induced. Some will make no sense to any of us. I will not change ANY words.

It is now seven years later and I am still heartbroken over the loss of my best friend. My daughter's father. There are songs that come on the radio that I can't listen to and there are times when I have to pull my car to the side of the road just to sit and cry. I spend a lot of days feeling like I've swallowed a hockey puck. The tears will well up and I find myself not being able to speak. We miss him everyday.

Chapter 2 (Matt's Story)

This is where Matt's story begins from his own journals, in his own words, his own writing. I have separated the days and times to try and make it more understandable. You will see by the photo copies that his journal entries were run on paragraphs with the dates and times mixed in. Just so you understand, some of the entries are missing dates.

My Story

2/25/2002 1:00pm – you have to change to change…take control of your situation. Think positive! Everything has a pos. and neg. side <u>always</u> look for the POS. trust God! Dear father, you know you are always the closest one to my heart, and I am soooo grateful to have you in my life but right now I need you more than usual. I need answers and guidance. Direction & strength. I'm not asking you to bail me out, I will always pay the consequences for my actions. So I will pray very hard and have faith that you will be done. Thank you Jesus!

6:10pm Hiding out in bedroom all day. Do not answer the phone! Need to talk to Teri lee bad! I don't know what to do. I guess just relax, don't stress, everything will be a lot better in the morning! (Here, he drew a smiley face) I'm not beating myself up over Joy, I think I did the right thing, weird! And that hickey on her neck! She will figure it out soon enough. Still haven't decided what to do about Dr.'s appointment on Tuesday. Waiting for God to decide. Time to start cleaning up shop, must call Teri. It sure was a beautiful day! I might just get some beer. O.K. I'm really starting to get paranoid. Got to call Teri!

7:25pm well it just keeps getting deeper, called Joy's, she's spun! From Bill, I guess everybody was trying <u>anything</u> to get dope, so Eduardo calls Terrilee supposedly about the phones, and ends up begging her for money. Can you fuckin believe that shit?! Then Joy accidentally drops the fact that she's waiting for some dope now. Lord give me strength! Then Ed goes down stairs & gets real drunk. Have I told you God how grateful I am for everything, thank you! So Teri lee's bringing some tacos over & who knows what she's heard. Woodland towers and residents are bad news! Give me strength. Don't answer the phone! I surrender. There shouldn't be ½ as much writing in here tomorrow… a lot less chaos. I must detach even from Terri if necessary. I hope she doesn't have any ideas about going over there. (drawn peace sign, a yin-yang symbol, a heart, a happy face and then a cross.)

One more time I'm unlocking the front door turning off the lights trying to crash! (I hope he meant locking the front door) I feel pretty shitty. Pretty soon that whole complex is going to get busted, I can feel it, I just pray that you keep me safe in my sanctuary where I belong…there's lessons and signs dropping all over the place. Must check B.G. 150.

11:05pm Teri lee to the rescue one more time. B.G. 309 chicken pie & oj. 25 units of "n". as I was saying Teri brings me my Sunday home cooked meal & finds me all thrashed in bed. I hated to tell her, but of course she lays down beside me and we talk. She doesn't preach or beat me up about it. We just talk. And as always I feel much better. I do realize that fear is warranted. I'm already back in active addiction. CAN'T MAKE IT TO THE MOST IMPORTANT DR'S APPOINTMENT BECAUSE OF THE TRACK MARKS ON MY ARMS. I think that's covered in the 1st step. So now what? HELP don't answer the phone! Stay away from Joy and Ed!!! Talk to Mark. Be careful! Easy does it, one day at a time, keep it simple…

all of that stuff. You have done it before, it's time to do it again.... now back to Teri, there really must be something special about me to deserve a friend like Teri, one more thing to be extremely grateful for. Once again God, all thanks to you. A little more writing then bedtime. Jessica your daddy loves you more than anything. I'm just going through some rough times. (he draws a heart).

2/26/02 – Yogurt, OJ 12pm B.G. 339. 15 units "r". Well, I made it back! Didn't get to sleep till late but I'll live. Now it's time to start taking care of business! I got a lot of stuff to take care of. Schauntell left message she broke up w/ Brian, I need to be there for her, POS people. I wonder what's up at Joy's? Chaos. Its time to give Marissa some much needed attention. Thank you Jesus! (drawn happy face). It's good to be back! Help me stay here. Beautiful day! Saw Schauntell, good energy, can't get out of Dr.'s appt. I guess that's how God wants it. My faith will get me through this. Going to eat something & crash.

3:30pm B.G. 249, 10 units "r" & sm. Sand & oj. Teri comes by, makes dinner, watch movie.

2/26 – Made it to appt. Bad feeling about it & I'm sure he saw my arm. Called J, he really made me feel a lot better!

3/2/02 – 7:30pm Nothing but eat & sleep the last few days! Ed stopped by tonight & cleared the fog. Teri puking all night my head aches. Joy called Ed hearing & seeing things. 5:00am must rest...

3/3/03 – 12pm well, spent from 5am to 10am with HORRIBLE migraine & severe nausea! Worst trip yet! Need help! Ouch. 4pm got a little food in me. Sm. Ish. Feeling little better. Teri's doing better than me. Beating myself up. In need of positive energy. Really getting concerned about problem. I'm sure there's a positive side to all of this. (drawn happy face) B.G. is way out of control. Just as you say about everybody else, you know what you have to do, you just gotta do it! Keep it simple. Don't eat too much.

Valerie Covert

3/4 – 1am made it through another day after. Barely. Told Joy I need to stay away. Hope tomorrow turns out better. Teri's still here, babysitting…comfortably numb, listening to live Pink Floyd & Enigma time to drift off into unconsciousness. Bye! Peace love and happiness.

3/5 – 10:50am up all night, got the pad cleaned & a few other projects done, Teri's snoring in bedroom, out of dope? Felt pretty good yesterday regained a little of my spirit back. Still lacking energy. It'll come. Back aches! Got a lot to do today, don't know if any of it will get done, but it'll work out (drawn happy face) I'll check back later…

5:30pm no sleep. Got the hook up from Joy, Billy & his girlfriend they came over and made breakfast & woke me up…you know…you can never depend on a binge to end so abruptly. Shit always happens! I have decided to keep my spiritual foundation, but as far as helping other people, I'm going to keep it simple & light. Like w/ Joy today, dope's not getting her high, but making her sick, tell her if it doesn't feel good don't do it. All I can do is tell her I care about her & have faith and a positive attitude & it will all make scents…cents? Everything is as it should be!!! But I'm still in the mix. Been up since Friday 4 days ago & eating a chicken pie & I'll be ready for action. Went to store w/ Billy he seems like and alright guy. Time to eat.. *8:30pm*, had a chicken pie & shower & shot for dinner. More collections notices on the mail, got the house spotless feels good to chill! Well I'm waiting for Chip to get here, 2 drug dealers hanging at Matt's sanctuary today. Losing control fast!! Think positive! Enjoy the lessons & watch for the signs! Be Careful! (drawn scared face)

10:20pm just had transaction with Chip he stayed a couple of hours. Really nice guy. Must get rest. Urgent! Can't see. Vision 85% gone. *12:35am* GodSmack LOUD (headphones) can't see but going to try writing this, spent 2-4 hours rearranging books on book case so I could fit all of my books on 1 case, after hours of measuring, stacking & restacking, comparing, I finally came up with the arrangement that would fit the absolute most amount of books in that amount for space. (Double Vision, seeing all kinds of shit that isn't there. Very enlightened and adventurous experience!) So, I came up with it, no more books could be made to fit in that bookcase. This morning when Joy & Co. were here, I counted the money I had in my hands 4 times and still couldn't tell you how much I had….Joy pressuring . trying to get me to come over. I say NO! I'm not leaving . Feel like I'm on a different world! (Cant explain, ask Tim Leary) almost a religious ex LSD? I've got some strange electricity (it's hard to spell rite when you can't see) going through my body. Need to be in my sanctuary alone to process & learn. Home is getting the <u>Energy Back!</u> Tonight is a good night to open my other eyes & take in everything I can.

3/8 – 8:05am A lot to write about! Starting where I left off. Woke up yesterday afternoon, slept good had big lunch, house was clean, had dope, money, ready to feel good! Joy calls & says it's Ed's B-day so we decide to get him something she says she's sending Betty to get me. By the time he gets here my guts are not feeling food so we wait a little while. I got the runs bad, Marissa had very good day though. But we make it to Joys! I just about shit my pants, make it to the car & no ass wipe! Wouldn't ya now?! The days adventure's got bad-trip written all over it. Bam! It rains CHAOS all over you as soon as you walk through the door. Joy's got John on the phone etc. So I go down to see Ed. I wake him up & we talk for while, I pray he gets better soon! We all do! We go back up to Joy's (CHAOS) everybody's getting high but me & Joy. I'm feeling her. We decide to go in her room & chill it's nice for a minute, the music gets louder, crank smoke in the air, tweakers everywhere. Ashley's in the kids room, painting, rearranging. Total Chaos! I <u>feel</u> Joy just loosing her sanity. I know she has to go through this stuff you have a very good reason for putting me there. Bad insulin reaction (I knew that would happen) so she gets the balls to tell her brand new roommates it's not working, Energy changes, Good! I finally talk her into going home w/ me for a few. I had to leave that minute. The night before, I had a good spirit recharge. But that house sucked it <u>all</u> out of me. We make it home. Thank you J. and I feel better instantly. So does she. Kick it for a few, do some dope, lots and lots of talk about hitting your bottom…not stuff you want to talk about when you want a good high. But the reality she's facing now.

I'm sure I didn't say the right things but I am fate and I'm sure my presence was needed. She's hurting and I'm feeling all of it. It's hard but she's getting closer everyday out of the 2 ½ years I've known her I've seen her grow more in the past month. Did a lot of dope, smoked some KGB talked about depressing stuff did more dope. I was saying silent prayers every chance I could & we survived another adventure. She took a Trazadone & I think she crashed, me, well I gave her a lot of my energy I guess I should go in there & lay down. I even thought about using my pump, but I don't think that would do anything but complicate things drastically! I probably won't be in my good place until I get some solitude & peace of mind but that's O.K. because that's my job. On a happier note Marissa was in rare form yesterday! Very Active! All over the house climbing & exploring. Her color looks good, I think it must be spring. Beautiful days! See Ya!

3/8/02 1:40pm Well Joy's still crashed. I'm done w/ all paperwork. Got a little peace of mind, talked to Teri. I think I didn't make much scents, but she knew where my brains were. Talked to Eduardo, he's going climb through Joy's window and make sure everything is cool. We really need to get him a present for B.D., still have lots to do, don't know if any of it will get done, but it'll work out fine. See Ya!

6:15pm Sex, Drugs & Rock & Roll words to live by. Ampin' Hard, pray for us all. Tonight I step over the line. But I have faith that your watching over me. While I'm watching over them. Well now after my 10 min break I'm off to Teri's house for chores. Wonder when my body's going to take a shit on me? Thank you Jesus! I need to fully recharge and everything will be peachy! I've taking care of business, it's cool! Se ya! (drawn chaotic face) Class is in. Pay attention & you my learn a few things, really good day. Got alot done, stressed out a little, everything worked out pretty smoothly, ended up with some alone time, good visit w/ Teri! Very enlightening, spiritual, soul back, made it home by 11pm. Relax. Pink loud in headphones held God in my arms! Spun on life, doing very little dope, always learning, 2:30am picking Joy up. Make it home. Not a great time. She's fighting it bad! It's time to back off. I'll follow your lead, you're the man! I love you Jesus

3/9/03 8am well just another nights sleep. Life is good! Have a few important things to do today. I'm sure Joy will see to it that were wired. I'm really getting the vibes, the end is near. Talk to you later. *11am* sitting on the toilet digging w/ my last ish, start puking & shitting at the same time, I really think it's time to stop! & I have things I have to do! I'm starting to think Joy's not ready, I have enough faith for both of us. I'll check in later, if I'm coherent. Strange, I'm feeling much better now. Except my vision is going now. Last night Joy says my couch smells like cat piss, I tell her it's her she swears it's the couch (it was her pants) then if that wasn't bad enough getting in bed she takes off her shoes and her socks smell like....well, very very bad! God please help her along. She really needs to know you're there.

3/9/2:45am I'm going for a record. I'm getting ready to crash hard! Even after a couple of ishes. My body is done! Joy ended going to John's for the night. I was actually a little sad. But I need this time alone w/ you guys. The vision is almost gone. I'll bet I've lost 30 lbs. Can't go like this much longer. I forgot. Joy turned over her apartment over to manager, the maintenance men go up & kick everybody out, including Ed. I'll bet it was a trip walking in on a bunch of junkies & spoofers most likely getting high. I'm proud of her I will pray hard for her. Eduardo on the other hand, I will pray hard for him, but I don't think we'll be spending much time together from now on. Joy did good but, somehow I ended up right in the middle of it we get back here there's a message from Ed (I can hardly keep eyes open) saying we better watch our backs, next things, my tires are going to get slashed. So we decide to celebrate & call Chip, Billy's friend & fellow CR salesman to trade some rigs, "went to pharmacy today" I believe this is the last. But Chip told Joy Billy & Ashley called him for a ride, as Chip was driving up he noticed Billy getting searched & I'm sure he had a whole lot of shit on him, so I'm thinking I doubt if Chip will ever want to have anything to do w/ us again. Not that we knew well, but he said he would come. So Joy takes off I pass out for a few, I'm cool I could just crash. But he showed up. Nice talk I like him I hope he doesn't think I'm gay. So he wants to quit too so we agreed that we would keep in touch. Maybe go to a meeting. Quiet night. I'm going to sleep now, finally, that bed's going to feel sooo good! Later.. (drawn happy face) love you Jesus. And my Princess

5:45 am not functioning in humanly way. Going in here hallucinations (he spelled hallutionnations) real real bad, I think I called at 4 am (Ed & Stacy) they were sleeping & think that made them a lot angrier. So I will call back (in daytime) if he talks to me good! If he doesn't I can't help it! I'm in a really good but spacey, different planet. Out of my mind.

3/10/02 – 12pm B.G. 297 Good Morning! Feeling much better so far, need to eat. My new neighbors have big dogs that bark a lot! This will be a real test to find something real positive about that, but I will. Beautiful Day. Spring is in the air. Joy hasn't called. Hope she's alright. Ed called a couple x's hope he's alright, it's about time for me 2 go MIA. I love you God! Talk to ya later…

3/11/02 – 12:02 am B.G. 165, homemade stew. Rest. Took care of a lot of stuff, preparing for the big day. Apparently that's not today. Went to Don & Ruth's, Don's going to be a dad! Got some green & a few tools, came home ready for the big sleep. Ed calls, ready for rehab, Thank You Jesus! So now we are here waiting for Chip. Oh Well, it's all good! Stupid tweakie stuff always organizing. Mellow. I'm very sore. I love you Jesus. 5:45am B.G. 572 25 units R must rest now. Laying flat on the floor. God Smack or Floyd on the phones LOUD!! Someday I would like a big room made just for listening to music Loud. The joy I get from it. Unfortunately the neighbors, I'm sure, are bothered by it & I feel guilty about it. I hope Henry the cat is OK. Watch over the whole family please God. (drawn heart, happy face and peace sign).

You know if this was thank you list for all the times that you reminded me that you're here watching over me guiding, teaching, answering all my prayers, I would need a lot more paper & pens. I'm still getting the new process, in my brain, I'm kinda thinking maybe I've done way to much good drugs & just snapped. I haven't written about it because Teri was teaching me slowly. So it kinda sneaks up on you. Maybe I should start from beginning. O.k. I'll start

MY SPECIAL PLACE

Dec 24, 2000 - (he got the year wrong here)Haven't talked to Teri in over. Jessica's in HI. Ready to take down x-mas decorations depressed & buzzed, bad connection. Eduardo calls me up reminds me we're gonna to spend x-mas together. If figured, why not? So he shows up in his mom's car SPUN. I had a few beers in me so I'm ready. Its on. Ed looks like he's been up for a few. Spoof. He throws a shit load in my spoon. I fixed it up. Did less thank ½ of what was in there. Anyway, first issue I've done in at least 7 or 8 months. I sit back on couch didn't feel anything for about 25-35 seconds, comes on slowly, mouth dries up, ears, ears, ears ringing. Heart thumping, dizzy & something I've never used to get an instant migraine. Extremely painful! Thinking that's would be a real bummer if Ed had to call 911, well he didn't thank God. Over amped I think, about 4 hours. The headache was starting it's fade, didn't do a whole lot but I'm glad I spent it w/ Ed. So he leaves for work that am. Leaves me $20 for x-mas. I saved a little of mine (dope) so I figure I'll do it later but it was just like the other times, I did it. It made me sicker than a dog, deathly ill, very very sick! See you later. (drawn pair of hands reaching up as in surrender).

So I suffered countless hours of misery, apologizing to Jesus, thinking he was a punishing God,. Made it through it all right beat myself up bad! Thoughts of suicide, etc. I've done this about 1 x a year, it always fucks me up. 2 days later I'm bed ridden, down for the count. Dec 28, Me & Val's anniversary. That's when it started & lasted till late Jan. that's when I started getting weak. Ed calling every day offering it. And I've been sick, not doing anything but, I'm feeling a little better, more energetic, but the mind of a tweaker you think it will make everything perfect. Wonderful. One Sat morning Ed calls from Joy's them with the bomb! I tell him bring it on. He get's here 1 ½ hours later with some thug looking guy. Chris, whom I later found

Valerie Covert

out, he is, nice guy though...Ed dumps it out, not much there, 3 fat lines, that's my new thing, just snorting it, that will make it work, going to help Ed move a little furniture into storage. Feeling good! A couple more later went back to W. towers, not long after Ed takes me home about midnight, tweaked had fun went all night long, felt pretty bad the day after. As usual. Not functioning, at all & my nose is completely plugged! Oh well, let's cure the insanity after 15 years of abusing this stuff and not finding a good way to do it. It just always makes me loose <u>everything</u>. So the next day I'm not dying but beating my self up really bad, need to confess to someone. Walking back from 7-11. Lookin thrashed w/6 pack of coors in hand, who do you think pulls over in front of me? Schauntell, there's my confession, she leaves, Teri calls, knows something is wrong Big Time. I guess I left some stuff out. I had been drinking at least a 6 pack of beer a day. Everyday! And sinking into a depression that I describe only as bad darkness, no hope, just thoughts. Lying to everyone. Sneaking it home, the whole deal. By Jan., I knew I needed help. So talking to Teri she says wanna talk about it, I say not now, she tells me she's bringing home cooked meal over tonight, when she gets here I unload on her, told all & we're talking about the high she decides she wants to try some. Far out. Always wondered what she'd be like. Not to mention, I was hating life, & just then Ed called said he had a ¼ left. We went & got it, I was actually feeling better. Ed gave me a little bit. We went home & agreed to sleep tonight & hit it early tomorrow. So I go up & do mine, not much, but it's Big Bill's stuff, A+ quality. Keeps me flying all night. The next day Teri doesn't show up until later afternoon and I'm thinking all kinds of weird shit, but here she is, lookin kinda amped. We do some fat rails & she says she's got to make dinner for her bro, who's in rehab, she'll be back later. So I'm spun now! Running a hundred m.p.h. Good High. She gets back later & we do more, I'm feeling guilty but she's a grown-up & just wants to experiment, so she starts talking, she knows my will to live has been weak lately so she's talking about positive thinking & glasses ½ full or ½ empty, processing and references, etc, etc. & I'm just trippin off her, I don't think it's the dope talking for her it doesn't all make sense but it's not buggin me, so I listen and every now and then remind her that I'm not sad & not going to off myself. But, I'm not afraid to die, in fact I'm anxious for *it to come, because I believe I'm through w/ my purpose on earth. She's got an answer for everything. So I listened & I listened we had a pretty good talk got some green bud she talked Don's ear off came home got buzzed, late, layed down in bed. Felt really close. Didn't sleep. Got up. Got high. Now 2 nights w/o sleep I'm feeling fair, eat chicken pies we do some stuff at her place & run some of my errands. I get sick for a minute. We come home, lay down in bed early am. Talking, holding hands, gently groping, well, I was any way. Nice day. A lot more of that cryptic talk about THERE or, my special place, talk talk . We end up ordering a ½ from ed for the next day but that night neither one of us had any dope for at least 12-16 hours. We had oral sex! Far out! Not bad though. She came about 5 times. No sleep, I'm feeling great, she's feeling no pain at all!!! Euphoria! No sleep she goes to take Rose to Food Locker, comes back just in time to meet Ed downtown, it's on now, back home many times more talk about - + & I say yea but I've always been a positive person, feeling like I always had been. She's counceling me on having a good high. We party talk do things, my house stinks like cigarettes bad! But I'm havin fun hanging w/ her. Binge last's about 5 or 6 days. & I crashed I think I stayed up longer! Joy & Ed stopped by to get me spun. So I come down & event hat was a pleasant experience. Sage, Rain, Clean house. Positive thinking. I'm feeling good. Real good, not high, not perfect & still – disabled. But in that place. Could that be it. I tapped into my soul & opened everything up? All in know is I feel good trying to help Joy & Ed. Don't know if it's drugs or selfish motives or what, I think it's pure love! So I've been discovering things all over, learning, seeing signs from God or nature or spirits, & being positive to every one I talk to. Something told me in the beginning to keep a journal & I did but I didn't know it would be for this, people are starting to notice my attitude, & so am I. No anxiety at all, no beating myself up. All kinds of things changing all the time. I realize it but don't question it. It's been sometime since we started this journey, a lot of good drugs, a lot of time spent w/ Teri, no more sex we decide, for right now. But I have gained ultimate trust w/ Teri, the real thing. So many things happening to me. Teri starts dropping hints about what's gong on in my head. To be continued. I can't put my finger on It exactly. Also it seem's that there are a lot of other people that at least know (or are themselves) your walking with* spirits. If it stays with me I guess I'll have a lot of study to do, another Beautiful Day! Might go to flea mkt w/ Teri. It's really a trip to interact when I'm in this condition (a couple of pipe his of the green) NO WHERE NEAR NORMAL. I love you God! Praise Jesus! Thank You ! One thing I can say for sure, it that I haven't had an anxiety attack or hardly any <u>stress</u> at all. The only stress I had was a couple outside situations that were very interesting lessons. It kinda makes me think go out today & see what you can learn out there! But now get up & eat something. Later… New writing utensils what fun (drawn happy face, cross, heart, peace sign, yin-yang symbol.

Hi again. Trying to get the hang of this new pen. A lot of new pens for journaling. 3/11 9pm So here we are Teri's talking up a storm, talking about our things, to be honest, I'm not likin the things I'm hearing, a person can only take being called a liar so many times before it gets to you. Ouch, the truth hurts, maybe I'm too fucked up to process all of this. Am I making sense? I guess I don't have it! That's BULLSHIT! I just need to get straight, think positive! Thank you Jesus, let me be your vessel. Schauntell and I when we pray we hit our target. Teri says that our prayers are lethal weapons & we should be careful with them.

Ok, focus. Get back on track. We're looking at my defects and there's a lot of them! Need to check yourself be pure. A day at a time. I hope every body's alright! I can't get into this now. Brain's fried. 1:25am did an ish. Feel a little better. Having problems with my eyes. Didn't get a lot done. I hope I get it back! I'm sure Teri's not going to let me lose what she gave me, she's working hard on me, and I can't see I must go. I love you all! Pray to have it back. 4am

3/12 11:30am B.B 60. well it's a beautiful day! A new day. My new neighbors dog barks too much! I need to learn to get peace from it. Well I think today is the day, I think I'm looking forward to it . something new. This woman, God bless her, can talk until your ears fall off. Thank you Jesus for all my blessings. I hope Ed's & Joy's angels are protecting them. (drawn happy face) I'm going to work *on my special place story as soon as I'm harmonized mind body & spirit. References! REFERENCE – ACT OR REACT = THE BIG PICTURE! Things are happening, my brain is working just fine. I love you Jesus. Revelation! When Teri used to talk about doing anything to improving her health & well being and I would automatically think about my health. I thought it was healthy to be at peace with your and accept your health problems & not try to make it better. Now I want to make the best of everything. Be the best I can be! I want to HELP people & the universe! Not for EGO, a year ago if I'd had the feelings that I do today, they would have come from the ego. I want to be the best at everything! For the betterment of everything and everybody. I love. I understand. I am no where near perfect, certainly no better than anybody else just different in my way. The special place (I think everyones got one) is inside me, I think we opened that door, I am still new at this but it's been about a month and a half but the changes that I've & other people Joy & Teri have noticed in me and are hard to ignore. The "signs & visions" could be blamed on the hallucinations, it's a gift, Teri calls it walkin in the light, I don't know how to explain it or it I should, I'm not trying to understand it. I'm just following God's will. I just have faith & do when it's right. When it happens a lot you will know, Ed & Joy I knew I had to help them. I just "did" & this is where it got me at this stage I can only speculate the outcome, in the beginning Ed was working & living, getting along with Ed. I <u>watched</u> him loose it all. He might not even be done now be he asked me for help. After a month and a half of chaos & insanity, dark evil times, I'm still learning, I've always liked Ed, but it's as if God is putting instructions in my head to help Ed & Joy, not to, sigh, only time awaits you 30 days in jail later only you awaits time.*

Pot, I've noticed has a bad effect on the capobilies(p). I don't want to get lost trying to describe how, why, who & where so I'm just gonna go w/ it. Teri says you wont forget any of it. I guess trying to capture it all on paper would be kind (my will) so for now I'm just chillin in a positive space, Marissa is in my reality. God bless. Do I have a resentment against Annas & Sharon & Willies church for leading me to believe that I must speak in tongues or have hands laid on me to have <u>real</u> faith? No but that is the ultimate mind fuck, here I am *trying to speak in tongues & beating myself up 4 not having enough faith. When all along it was <u>all</u> in my heart & soul. But Im sure not many people share in my beliefs, views, live & let live.*

3/12/ 6:30pm Well, Teri"s gone, all alone except Marissa & she's going crazy trying to climb out windows & eat plants. The hour is drawing near. That was nice of Teri for the pens as I'm confident you noticed I'm using a fountain pen. I'm waiting for some dope to show up that's the way it's been working but, maybe he's going to stop it. I like letting him run things. Less to worry about. Well I must also get something out. At times I was thinking some evil stuff about Teri. Talking too much, bragging, etc. She is an Angel & I often forget that. I don't know where those thought were coming from. Teri would say ego. But I got over it, prayed about it, all better. Hope Ed & Joy & everybody is blessed. Another thing as I'm sure you know, I may skip a few days of journaling hopefully not as these will be many lessons to learn in the coming days. But if not have faith, think positive, and all the other sayings that go along with it. See Ya!

11:00pm Well here I am. Let me be the first to admit that I'm having a hard time. I think this is going to be just a little rougher than I anticipated. Well, I'll live, Praise Jesus!!! Thanks. I kinda wish we could go back, still don't know what happened to Joy? Watch over her God. About to try something different, SLEEP. Tomorrow will be fine. Hopefully as beautiful as today. I didn't leave the pad. It's the unknown out there! This sure has been one of the most interesting 2 mos of my life. I guess that why I wanted to get it all down but so far everything just worked out. God willing it will continue to do so. Yea, I'm still here, don't give me any shit! I really like my new pens. Good night! (drawn happy face) I'll try to write tomorrow. No promises. (drawn peace sign)

3/13 12:30am. B. G. 369 I know I probably boring the crap out of you. 5 units R 9 units NPH. I feel very unusual, on my way down, down that road again, but, it's different this time. Can't put my finger on it probably cause I'm stoned out of my mind! Vision extremely bad.

Burnt hard. I can't help wishing some dope would come by. God is going to make this a painless procedure, I'm gonna go pass out now. I love you.

3/14 – Day 1 Joy called & on her way over feel very strange?

3/15 Day 2 well, a lot happened yesterday, Ed came over Joy stayed for a while until John <u>made</u> her leave. Talked to Roger a few times. Got Ed on unemployment, called some recovery places. I think Ed is too tired to do anything or just isn't ready. I'm trying to see through the fog, but, it isn't easy at all! I'm taking baby steps, need to pray more. And check my mail! Let go & let God. Joy called again this am looking for a place to hang out. I need answers I feel like God is taking a break w/ me, what, is it, do I have to be spun to be connected with him & my spirit? Please help!! I'm here. Reach out! See you later.

5:30pm well, my house is mine again! Payed Ed's storage, took him back to Stacy's got a few groceries & now I'm going to sleep! Marissa's ok still haven't checked mail but oh well! Feeling a little physical discomfort (to be expected) see ya...

3/17 12:35pm Yesterday was a trip. Joy's negative attitude finally getting to me. We took Ed down to AOD, I didn't need to be there! It went really well! Val had a boob job, I couldn't stop thinking about her. I miss her & will always love her! Got my spirits back in order semi-grounded. I love you Jesus! 5 messages from Joy. She got money. Has to go to assessment at heritage oaks, I'm not up to it, so Terilee's taking her. I think that's what's supposed to happen. I tell her if Teri says it's ok we'll get some dope? Marissa's all over the place. I feel good. Need to talk to Valerie & Jessica! (drawn happy face)

(drawn happy face) 4:50pm UP again. Chip came by. Teri & Joy doing some soul searching. Me, just observing. Talked to Valerie & Jess. Val doesn't sound to good. I let her know she's in my thoughts. Now what? Shower maybe. Talk to you soon. I'm sure I'll have plenty to

write about. Joy thinking of sending Sammy to Randy's (drawn mad face)! Is that for me or you to decide? Please help on this matter... Colors, Blue = sky, Dk Green = Earth. So far so good. (drawn happy face) understanding. God you are good! I'm on the outside looking in ... talked to Hank and he e mailed Yvonne, far out! Joy's going through it. I hope I'm not hurting her. I'm feeling a little bit queasy. "I'll live". Watched Magnolia, too much for my frame of mind. BG has been ok. Marissa pooped in the kitchen today. Oh, by the way, I love you!

3/18 1:50pm. O.k. not such a good idea! It's a crap shoot, it's 50/50 good trip, bad trip, well, we're on the latter of the two. Shit happens. Joy & Teri talk all night, I get sick, I throw the dice, now I pay the price. Beautiful day! Thank you Jesus! Actually I'm stoned & feel tolerable, really need to do something positive. No more thinking! I wonder why the first day up always fucks me up so bad? Well, Mumbo Jumbo poor me. I think it's time to stop and stay stopped and <u>if I can't do it by myself,</u> "and it looks like I can't" GET SOME FUCKING HELP!!! Had close time w/ Joy, have absolutely no idea if I'm good / bad / right / wrong, just going to be now. BG way out of control! Dehydrated, can't think of much positive stuff to write, but I'm trying hard! See ya! (drawn frustrated face). I surrender!

1:42am BG 40 Chaos all day, I can't take it anymore. 3 nights ago Joy stayed at John's. I missed having her in my bed, I woke myself up yelling for my dad having a very real nightmare, holding Joy in my arms in bed, she holding a knife shaped like a crucifix, trying to stab me in lower back...was that a sign? (JOY ACTUALLY DID STAB MATT ONCE IN THE LEG WITH A PAIR OF SCISSORS) Chaos, Chaos, David picks her up, peace of mind. I call Teri, Val & Jess & lay down! Heaven aaahhh good night. I do still love her, but must do it from afar...

3/19 10:45am Thank you Jesus, good night sleep, peace of mind & serenity. It's all good now. Chores to do. Must call & thank Teri. talk to you soon. I love you. The dogs barking next door remind me

The Bottom is Six Feet Under

that there's a pretty girl with dark hair living there. Hey! Guess what? My heads in a really good space, Marissa's even calmer. I had faith, thanks. I hope everything went ok with Joy this am. I'm sure it went the way it was meant to go. To much noise & chaos over the weekend. Chip drops by to do an ish with me, good stuff! Good visit. B.S. for a long time. Got all my little chores done. Joy's on another mission. Lied to her so I could enjoy the high, which I did until about 4am when all the sudden I got violently ill & vomited in the kitchen sink. I felt al lot better afterwards. Drugs? Never know what to expect. It's now 3/20 11:05am, been up, need a shower, Marissa's going crazy. Just talked to Joy, she doesn't sound very good at all! Henry (Cat toy) ran away from Pats. Joy read me some stuff from Kyle's monster book, real trippy. It's time to get that lizard out and take a fucking shower. Bye. Thank you Jesus! I'm grateful! No see, just called Chip, I'm powerless, your in control God. But it is a Beautiful day & I have clean shorts to wear.

4:05pm waiting for Chip to call back, somebody else answered his phone, I'm thinkin he's over at Stacey's if so I would really be knee deep in CHAOS, Chip's "I'm sure" very discrete. Joy sure let me have it. (or tried) I think I handled it o.k. Schauntel came by. I took the cowards way out and didn't answer the door, but I think she saw me through the kitchen window. I'm stoned but I think I'm understanding that one now. Here I am saying I need help, just now I realized how bad I am. She was my help, my Angel & I hid from her. Because I'm waiting for Chip to call. Dope is the only thing on my mind! Already thinking of canceling my dentist appt. That's 2 days away, I guess you could say the drugs controlling me. I have faith in you Jesus! I love you. (drawn frustrated face) I'm o.k. B.G. are wacked, barely any food...don't know if I should call Chip or Schauntell? Both hard calls to make. Comfortably numb...Chips on his way, with Shawn, the skinhead felon. I'm powerless over my addiction & my life is becoming unmanageable....

3/21 3am Chip finally made it by. We did an ish & shot the shit awhile. He gave me a few CD's (drawn happy face) I really enjoy his company, unfortunately, he's a little to generous with the dope. Joy got mad earlier because I can't be around her when she's jonzing, depressed, negative, etc. so I haven't heard from her since early afternoon, peace & quiet. I'll bet on a normal day she calls at least 15 times, that phone drives me nuts! Jesus please look after her & all the kids. Walked to 7-11 beautiful night, hotter than Hell up here today. Summer's on it's way! So I'm waiting on a pot pie, haven't been eating well at all. Getting sucked up, talked to Schauntel, it was a sign. On the 28th her & me & Teri, maybe a couple others are going to have a real GURU & his wife come up here (my pad) & talk about our spiritual stuff, all of it. $15 a head. I swear I hear that phone ring even when it's turned off. Ok. Going to eat & ? Love ya.

3/21 3:50pm B.G. not good. Not feeling too bad. Don't start enjoying it till the third day. No phone calls for at least 3 hours, knock on wood, hands hurt bad from steel wool, , guitar & chemocols.. cemachols, use the damned dictionary. Could have sworn I heard a girl calling my name? I rescheduled Dentist appt. lots of chaos going down at the Towers, It's not my job to get involved with that negativity, so I got my house mostly in order. Teri's going to come pick me up and I'm going to take a mini vacation, maybe get some work done, need to call family!! Talk to you soon...(drawn picture of face with beads of sweat)

4:30pm on toilet. Pot pies going right through me. This is the kind of BM that waits for NO MAN! Glad we weren't out and about. I'm ready for a swim and a ride in the pm in the MGB..bye...

7:20pm B.G. 148, two pot pies, Teri into conversations with you book so I might be a home body tonight. Double vision bad. Can't hardly write. Was that you that made my phone quit ringing? Thanks...I think I might shower and go to Dimple.

3/23 7am – it started thursday or Friday when Teri took Jon to hospital & I did sleep one night. I'm *very* stoned! I don't know how long since I have slept. I think I misspelled it? Not much left! I'm thinking if I do as many positive, no wait, maybe I was looking at the glass ½ empty. My vision is so bad it's FREAKING me out.

Hey, I do believe, honestly, here and now, I am loosing my mind. Little negative things happening, CD player not working, talked w/ Schauntel, PASSED OUT!

3/22 – 10:15pm Lots of strange things going on, probably don't have time to write all of it now, or weather it's worth writing. I'll try. First and foremost, Marissa's sick. She looks bad! If she dies I don't know what I'll do. Eyes already going bad. Good things got groceries. Grapes for Marissa. Got Gary Newman CD, worked on bike, Teri's my fried! Joy sober and back w/ John. Can't wait to ride my bike.

3/24 9:45am Yep, you guessed it... another all nighter & I was going to write you before I toked. I forgot so I don't know when I'm going to pass out... ya know the shit I pump into my tired, scarred up veins is such a lethal dose of toxic poison, chemicals you could ever imagine. Why I continue to substitute my blood. Eyes going bad. That "death in a spoon". I just don't get it. I think if chemists made this shit 75 years ago, something that takes <u>everything and everyone good</u> away from you and puts you in jail and kills you and kills you and everything negative you can think of. And I drop a little more in the spoon. If they can make something so bad, so addictive, why the fuck haven't they invented a cure for cancer? I'm wondering if enough is coming out of my pores that Marissa's problem is that I've just kept her spun, that is kinda what she looks like. All thrashed. Weird look in her eyes. Paranoia, no eat, no sleep. Dehydrated. Sketchy. Her and I experience the same side effects. I'm too fucked up to be scared. Spending a lot of time thinking about suicide. I would have to be in this drug induced state of mind when I did it. Would be a trip of course. Everything's a trip when you're in this state of mind. Ok. Enough of this BS.. Marissa's acting very strange! I'm really fucking worried about her, more and more I feel like I'm going to snap and loose my sanity all together but God if you take her away from me now, I guarantee that I would end up in SMIC (5150) (that's my muffin) I can't seem to stop crying. I'm always afraid somebody will see. Don't really give two fucks if they see now. I am so lost. I could have go to sleep about 12 hours ago, I'm straining to stay awake. Right now, is there something I enjoy about this feeling? But if Chip came by now w/ issue I would gladly do one his amount. Still haven't found my stash. I don't know if I just dreamed all that or what? I've got a lot of writing to do & I just caught myself writing with my eyes closed so I must die for a while. I love you Jesus...

3/24 2:30PM. Last two days kinda a blur, passed out this am. 1 ish left. Talked to Chip last night, told him not to give me any more dope. It was easy to do when I was spun. God help me stick with it! I'm sure Teri will be around to help. Marissa's still not eating. But she looks better. Maybe, we're just coming down together. Shauntell came by yesterday, recharged me a little. I think she's gonna help me. Talked to mom (1st time in 2 weeks). I guess Joy's sober w/ John. Good luck. Today is the first day of the rest of my life! Thanks J. Time to think positive. Prepare for the trip down. I know there's so much I wanted to write the last two days. Interesting and terrifying personal journey. I'm thinking I wasn't supposed to remember those things, in any event, I got a little sleep & food. Not totally prepared, but it's time. Need to pray hard! Keep calling Jess. Take care of self and Marissa. God willin she's gonna be alright. Gonna eat. TCB. Talk to you later...

3/26 8am. Just woke up. Had cereal yesterday. Doing little tweaky things & nodding off occasionally. Ed and dan came by to get mail & rig. Big ish of Bill's stuff. Dan spun! I split mine w/ Teri, still a little bit left in rig, don't know what to do with it? So, yesterday, early pm, started feeling queasy, laid down for a few, started raining hard, smells good & fresh. Wake up about 9pm. Shit my pants. Go to bathroom. Before that, had a <u>BAD</u> insulin reaction drank 3 lg cups of OJ, 2 cans Vienna sausages, 3 twinkies. After my shit went out to living room feeling very nauseous. Teri seems to be okay. I go back to bathroom, shit and projectile vomit at same time. Go back to bed. Teri says she's leaving. I actually got a little scared. Mostly because I need her to watch Marissa. So she stayed. I told her I miss doing the fun we used to do like garage sales, etc. Even cleaning the boy's bathroom would be more fun than that! This am Marissa ate a few grapes & drank a little water. Please God, don't let her die! Please!!! (it's time to make my house a home again.) it's only been about 3 months since I started this binge (or since I became a junkie again), *but I don't even remember what it was like before this all started, nor do I know if I'll ever be the same. I've learned a lot about myself & others. Transformed my spirituality to a more higher level, tweaked, polished and organized EVERYTHING in my house. My hands are raw with infected cuts all over them. Many people have shot dope in my bedroom. There's not a lot of good energy here now. I'm not saying there wont be, but it's going to take a while & Marissa to get better, I'm going to come down and if I can't I'm going to find a way to end my life. This one. That's a way I can still get to Heaven & Dad & Henry the Dog...talk to you later..love ya and thank you for the rain last pm. & for waking up feeling good. & especially for my friend Terilee. Bye. (drawn happy face)*

3:45 starting my journey downward, must think positive! It won't be bad, plus I put a call in to Chip, he'll call right before I start hurting bad. The house is clean, Teri gone & said if I need food to call. I talked to Ed. I guess Joy & John broke up, IMAGINE THAT! And she's jonesing. We'll I'm going to burn some sage, pray, take a shower, pray again & maybe make some cookies, if you don't hear from me, it's probably a good sign. Bye. (drawn happy face)

5pm just wanted to report, somebody stole the small bottle of Eternity out of the bathroom, I know It's my fault, I'm just writing so I can forget about it. Still hanging in there.

7:15pm Everything smooth so far, praise God. Getting ready for bed. Full stomach, thank you Jesus! The moment of truth is upon us. God stay with me please. THINK POSITIVE! KEEP IT SIMPLE, ONE DAY AT A TIME! KEEP THE FAITH! It's going to be nice to get back to normal. Wish me luck. Goodnight. (drawn ¼ moon with smiling face)

3/26 10:20am. HI. Loaded. Feeling really chipper, first day off, probably high off of what's still in my system. Marissa still not eating much. Going to try new routine, play & exercise & eat in the morning, basking in tank in afternoon???? I feel <u>real</u> good right now!!

Valerie Covert

    3/27 11:40am Oh shit! Here come the tears. Day 2, Marissa still not eating. (Illegible) called. I wonder if somebody's been talking to her? It's weird knowing that people really care about you…thank you Jesus!

    3/28 Day 3 – Ed comes by. Teri brings McDonalds. I get sick & puke.

    3/29 Day 4 – Lots of sleep & food & prayer. 3pm Teri bringing food & cheer & Rolaids, I just don't know why she takes such good care of me. Thank you Jesus for such a good friend.

    3/30 Day 5 – 9:55am Thank you Jesus! Teri & Ed pickin me up to go to Woodland T. I just told Marissa if she ate a grape I'd let her out and she did. Anyway, I'm feeling quite well this am. Love ya. 3:15pm took a shower! Feel good. Shauntell here w/ new car. Karrie called, doesn't look like Chip is going to call. Life is good! Love you Jesus!

    3/31 11:00am – well Chip came by last night got me spun! Talked w/ Sue. She said nothing to worry about. Marissa's gravid, I need to make her a nest. Been up all night. Supposed to go w/ Teri to Roseville Auction & meet Tom. How am I going to pull that one off? Went for a ride in Shauntell's new car. It's nice. Time for a road trip. Mark & Kevin moved out. No more squeaky floors. Ed's been ringing off the hook! Well, I'm going to either relax or get something done, pot pie in oven. So I think I'll try to chill…talk to you later. (drawn frustrated face) I still have the faith…just talked to Teri, she doesn't feel good. No auction today! I'm sure she knows about my current condition… 2:45pm Chillin. What I wouldn't give to wash the MG, put the top down & go for a long drive. Built a nest for Muffin. She's shown some interest, but right now she's sitting on top of it. I guess only time will tell? I wonder if Teri's going to be mad when I tell her, probably not if I save her some, who knows? I'm not going to stress about it. Oh, by the way, thank you Jesus for everything! I'm extremely grateful for everything, even the difficult lessons. For some reason, I feel very close to you right now, a very good feeling! I love you Jesus! You are my savior. I know I sin & I want to repent those sins. Please hang out with me for a while longer... (drawn happy face, heart, ying-yang, peace sign, cross). Ok. I better do something, even if it's wrong. Later.

6:48pm Well all in all, it's been a pretty mellow day, phone didn't ring much. Teri's bringing some chicken over, I got a little laundry done, haven't heard from Tom yet. Just takin a breather. Mild headache. Everytime I do an ish I get really nauseous, maybe that's a sign? Sure did some bell ringers last night! God give me the strength to stop after this. In Jesus name! Bye...oh by the way, it's getting really hot! Lots of sweat! Dying for a swim. (drawn fish with bubbles)

4/1 6:25am April Fools' Day. Daylight savings time. have not done a lot of dope, good high though. Chips private stash. Little beer & weed buzz. LOUD Creed in headphones, clean clothes, I'm almost really enjoying being spun. But this is the one in four or five that I don't have a bad reaction (get sick) really enjoyed hanging out with Chip. Sean's a trip. Got to ride in a stolen car. Thank you Jesus! I hope Marissa gets normal soon. Need to send Jess a card! Talked to Ed & Joy last night. Eduardo called & asked if I would talk to her! I thought he 3 wayed me! I was really loaded. Turns out he had his mom leave him there. He's spun cleaning Joy's apt. I laughed real hard. Actually had a real good chat w/ both of them. Of course, neither of them know anything about what I've been doing. Apparently Chip is equally discrete. I think I could hang out with him sober. The sun comes up a lot sooner. Far out, can you dig it? Put your head down & your ass in the air! (one of his dad's famous sayings) ok, I guess I've babbled long enough, one cool thing about writing I can talk as much as I want & I wont make an ass of myself. Bye. Thank you for the peace of mind (drawn happy face and sun).

10:35am Hello. Still doing well here. Thank you very much! Waiting on Teri. Marissa woke up went into kitchen & took a crap! Oh well, at least she has something to poop out. Gotta go.

Valerie Covert

9:30pm All goes well. Knock on wood. (drawn frustrated face)

4/2 10:25 am Chip came by last night 2 do an ish, I let him leave some stuff here, which is probably a mistake? I think he's thinking he can do a fix here whenever he wants, and I'm sure I did nothing to lead him to think otherwise. God, I'm really needing some help here. A night of projects gone bad. Did put new strings on guitar & had a good talk w/ Jess. YEA! She's my princess! Passed out about 5am w/ candles lit, woke up at 9:30 candle wax all over guitar bookcase & carpet...oops. Woke up with severe dope hangover, took 45 minutes to fix...arm sore but feel a little better now. Going to start my day now. Bye. Praise you. My father. Please help! (drawn happy face) 1:35pm Schauntell came by and beat on the door yelling and calling my phone at the same time. feeling a bit ill at the moment. Pot pie in oven, lg cup OJ, don't know if it's different dope, just burnt out or high B.G. Who the fuck knows? Who cares? 1:30 in the afternoon & I can't imagine going out in the public. Sure hope I feel better after some food! gonna chill for a few. I would Schauntell would call back cause I gotta make some make some calls & I don't want her to call & it be busy. After she beat on my door for 20 minutes. I might even call Joy & see if she'll come over. I shaved my balls yesterday & I'm really glad I did. It actually feels really good & clean, just in case you were wondering. I'm thinking Schaunells not going to call back. This hiding from people just aint right. Be back later...(drawn heart)

3:30 Schauntell came back. Sat in her car, then Teri pulls up. I thought she would use her key, but they stayed down there and I hid up here, quiet as a (illegible) mouse. Talked to DDS, hopefully they wont drop me! Talked to Joy. Invited her over for a while. Must shower & pay rent. Very important! Creed is extremely good sounds! Marissa's not looking good today. Bye.

10:20pm CHAOS GALORE over the phone, when I hung up the chaos stayed over there. Time to settle down. Thank you Jesus from delivering me from making that mistake. Jesus I totally accept you as

The Bottom is Six Feet Under

my savior. And except that I am living your will but please help w/ the drug problem!! Gotta call Jess. Bye.

Hi, it's very late or very early, I can't figure out which it is? Who cares? You may have guessed from my writing that I had a couple Coors & a little green. Not spun. It's funny, when I can get it free everyday I tend to use a lot less. Come down more. Actually plan on sleeping every night. It's still fuckin me up Bad! No matter how I try to use it I get real sick or at <u>least</u> 60% of the time. I'm sure my blood glucose will never be the same but I have all the faith in the world whatever's going on is what is supposed to be going on, for the most part. At least, a lot of times, when I try to do something my way, I usually get a pretty good signal from you…telling me it's time to check myself. Tonight Joy was asking why I <u>really</u> wanted her to come over. She was drilling me about it & me being stoned couldn't' think. She thought it was because I wanted her dope! If she only knew!! I guess I can understand where she's coming from. Laying here now, I realize I wanted a female companion. Someone I can hold, kiss, maybe intimate, maybe kinky, and if the circumstances are just right, she's the only one I can think to do that with. & I'm thinking now that I'm sure I'm alone tonight for my own good. Well, I sure hope Eduardo makes it out to Galt ok tomorrow! I'm almost jealous. Man, do I have a problem! Plus constant, severe heartburn! But I'm going to cra (I THINK HE MEANT TO WRITE CRASH BUT DIDN'T FINISH THE WORD).

4/3 1:20pm – Well, here I am, sitting on the John. Last night when I was writing I felt ok and then all of the sudden I got these horrible chest pains! I couldn't even finish my sentence, blew out the candles and passed out. Woke up about noon feeling very hungover, had a can of soup, some OJ & ginger tea & sm ish. Currently taking a very large and satisfying BM. Feel ok though. Thank you Jesus for getting me through last pm. Bye.

10:24pm Real good day! Except Marissa is looking real bad today. Must call Sue tomorrow. If she dies it's going to really fuck me up!

Called a lot of friends today. Cindy said I could use her guitar. Talked to young James (still a delinquent) got some projects done. Very little dope. Schauntell brought her chicken & dumps. Very good. I was getting ready to go through Chip's backpack when he called and said he was en route. For once he had been up & looked thrashed & I was in good shape. He brought Jack-in-the-Box. I don't mind seeing him all the time, I just wish he would be less of a drug dealer. But I except people for what they are, I guess that's one of the things that makes it cool that he comes by all the time. (The big dealer comes by just chill & bring food, free drugs & CD's). How much better can it get for a junkie? RECOVERY! Gotta call Jess. Bye.

4/4 9:48am BG High. Been extremely spun all night (MULTITASKING) going nowhere very fast! It just kinda crept up on me. I think I'm trying to escape my feelings about Marissa. If she dies I don't know what I'll do. (drawn sad face). I need to call Sue. I wish I had slept. My back is hurting real bad, vicodin doesn't even phase it. Very confused. Can't think straight at all!! Going to shut my eyes 4 a while. Watch over Marissa and everybody. Bye.

2:14pm – Kinda had an emotional break down this am. I guess denial finally wore off. Marissa is really sick! Cried for a long time! called Sue 1st thing this am and she said to get her to the vet now, so at 4:30 she's coming to pick us or her up. You see it seems I accidentally stayed up last pm on some sketchy dope, and I'm definitely not up for being out in public. I can't believe this woman, paying her vet bill, her heart must be the size of a basketball! Thank you Jesus & thank you Sue! (illegible) left a message that she's worried I may have relapsed, I'm now gathering up the COURAGE to call her & ask for help or make a Big Mistake. Man, I'm thrashed, gotta go, the adventures of my life continue. I'll keep you posted. Bye. (drawn frustrated face)

4/5 4:40am. Yes I'm going to sleep. Let me just start out by saying, words alone cannot describe the love & gratitude that I have for you right now Jesus! My Muffin's going to be all right!!! Not only that, you put someone so special in my life, again words cannot describe how special this lady is, not much more than strangers, Sue picks me up and I am very thrashed! She takes Marissa and I out to her vet. Keep in mind, I was convinced Marissa was dying and there was nothing I could do about it. The vet examines her & almost gets bit in the process, I told her about my not perfect Iguana home & she's telling me that if the temperature isn't perfect, they will get all messed up, which is probably true in some cases, but like I've been saying she was totally content. Happy, healthy, lazy & regular. So they take x-rays & blood. Anyway, so far, they say she's HEALTHY. I still have to find the results out today but I have faith in you, Marissa, Sue, the vet, people have been very good lately, coming out of the woodwork to support & help me in every way. It was a trip looking at her x-rays & all those little eggs in her. Ok. I'll finish the story later. have to crash now. Goodnight. Thank you Jesus!

4/5 1:40pm Thank you Jesus! So far it's been a great day! Ate, cleaned talked on phone cleaned some more. Bill & Ashley back at Joy's, go figure. Marissa wakes up at 1pm – feeling good, looking good & a little good food. Well I'm thinking about calling (illegible) in fact, I'm going to now. Talk to you later…

9:15pm Eyes BAD! Called (illegible) today had a very encouraging talk. She's going to help me get clean! I can't thank you enough for putting such great people in my life! You are my savior! Good day. Billy, Ashley & Joy came by for a rig & game of darts. Billy won. Ed wants to know about storage? I have about an hour to let him know, all in all, it's been a pretty productive day. Felt real strange tonight. Double vision! (illegible) of course the amount of dope I do is so small I sometimes wonder if it's all in my head anyway. Shitting out my dinner of Top Ramen. Oh, I forgot to mention Joy, Billy and Ashley coming by to get me wired. The first sign of chaos everybody leaves!!! I would rather wait for it than deal w/Chaos to get it, but it has been kinda lonely around here, I am becoming a hermit. Change is coming soon! Ok. Gonna get off the john…bye…

4:20am 4/6 – Don't know what time vet appt is? Don't forget to get details on feeding Sue's Iguana's. Well, I probably should have just went to bed, the gang came over for darts & issues. DO NOT LIKE that many tweakers in my home. Or any for that matter. But I survived. Joy was the most annoying out of all of them. Man, what a drag she is. I don't know why she even does dope. It just makes her more miserable. I sure hope she figures it out soon. I think I've got Ed's storage taken care of. I might drive his mom out to see him. Bless him & everyone for that matter. I guess it's time to crash. My blood sugar is worse than it's ever been. I wonder what that's doing to my body. Ok, well, goodnight or good morning whatever? I love you Jesus!

4/7 2am Everything good today! So far! Marissa to vet today, SSI hearing on the 18th! I've got faith. Made plans w/ Teri to tweak on her house, I'm so tired of tweakin on my house alone. Not a lot left to do here. Rearrange speakers & MGB. Important projects, Ed should be out at Altua Village now. Right on Ed! Better go now, bye (drawn happy face).

4/7 4:50pm – SPUN! All night w/ Teri. Chip's private! Talked a lot! Did a lot. A lot more to write. Multitasking now talk to you soon, I love you!

4/8 8:16am Couple hrs of sleep, kitchen spotless! Food & good ish last night really mellow! Teri laid down & stopped talking & I did my thing. New start, house looks new! going to try to get early start, get some stuff done at Teri's. If she'll stop talking long enough. Screamin dope! Ok. Gonna go now, talk to you later. Thank you & I love you Jesus…(drawn happy face)

4/9 5:15am Good morning Jesus. I need to talk to you, sorry I haven't written much, as you can see I've been a little out there. Not as bad as Teri, yesterday, she was so out of it she fell down in front of her house, BAD! I know she's a big girl & can take care of herself, but I still feel responsible in a way. She was way out there. Way different than the Teri I know & love. Got some things done today. But didn't have any fun. I've decided that I very much don't like Teri when she's on it. I'm starting to think a lot of her talk is just babble. Crank gibberish. I do believe some of it is her beliefs but when she's wired, she just lays on the couch & smokes & <u>talks,</u> talks, about the same things over and over and over. When I leave the room she keeps on talking. When she's by herself she talks to herself, if she's not talking spiritual she's talking about how rich her family is and bragging about how special she is & how, oh ya, know what? I love her w/ all my heart, I think she just shouldn't do crank. I got a whole lot done this weekend and she did absolutely nothing done but smoke a lot of cigarettes and tell the same stories over and over again. Of course, I have learned from it all, I think I'm going to pass out, so see ya!! Love you

4/9 11:19 Hi, a lot of sleep this am. Couldn't wake up. When I did I was in bad shape! Panic, confusion, sickness, etc. called Teri no help there. She's delusional, made a few calls, she's going to take Marissa to Vet. Chip coming by, Teri on her way to take me 2 get food stamps & pay bills. Starting to stress! We ½ way there, Teri starts yelling, irrational!! Stress level high! I take care of this ASAP, come home & Sue's waiting w/ my muffing. (drawn happy face) things are mellowing out a little. Chip gets here, with enough dope for 1 ½ ishes. I'm dope sick! So is he, quick fix. All better. Do I love or hate being a junkie? God, please grant me my SSI please! Anyway, Chip takes me shopping (no food) he doesn't realize he's got a rig sticking out of his shirt pocket. Got too much junk food. Drops me off says should have more dope by 9. calls at 10:30, no go until tomorrow. Almost can't function without it. He did leave me his bike, very nice Specialized. So mellow night. Dinner, few beers, talked to Jess. Bedtime. Eyes going to quit soon, better go. I love you Jesus! I'll pray soon.

4/11 6am Well, I guess you figured out that I wasn't sober yesterday, until about 11pm. Chip came by w/ an ish, weird stuff, or maybe the fact that I ate & slept all day. Who knows? Well, I'm tripping bout the SSI thing! Marissa goes to the vet for 3 days. I don't know what I'm going to do with out her around here. I don't know what I'm going to do without Teri either. Hopefully I won't have to, we'll see. Going to try to get chip to come by here before work 4 a dime or so. Don't know how that's gonna go? I hope you got the prayer Schauntell & I sent your way. I'm really going to try hard to go for a bike ride today. I think it will relieve a lot of stress & right now I have a lot of stress! I sure am glad I have you Jesus! It seems like you're the only one I have these days. Ok. I'm gong to call Chip, or crash now. I'll talk to you soon! I love you! (drawn happy face)

4/11 11:15 am Chip came by, on his break dropped off a very large dime. Ann called. Talked to Teri she's going to take me to lawyers office tomorrow. It sounds like she's herself again. Thank you! Gonna run now. I love you!!!

2:20 Sue came & picked up Marissa, she looked scared, not going to see her until Friday. I'm going for my first bike ride. I'll write later & tell you how it was…(drawn peace sign, heart and happy face)

Hi, it's 10:15pm. The only call I've had was Joy. To tell me I need to get sober. No – shit! Just say no, right? So she's got a couple of days of sobriety and she's fixed, shed cured herself, the only reason she's not spun is nobody will give her any. Ok. I just had to let that out, well I got a few things done around here. Fixed Teri's battery charger & charging MG battery I think I got batt. Acid all over my clothes. I feel pretty relaxed right now thank you for that! Now I'm counting on you to be there w/ me tomorrow! I'm going to take care of the foot work, you handle the results. Rode the bike about ½ mile. In the wind. Almost killed me. Nice bike though. I sure hope I'll be able to tell the judge how I feel. Maybe I should bring notes to the hearing definitely take notes at meeting tomorrow! Chip just called to see how I was doing. Nice chat. Say's he's got some new stuff if I want to try it I said probably tomorrow. I think I'll really him when I get sober. That's another thing I keep skirting around, is recovery. What the hell am I going to do, if I get SSI, Rehab & I am God willing going to get it, so just plan on rehab. Alright, I'm going to mellow now, talk to you later.

The Bottom is Six Feet Under

4/12 1:45pm Crashed at 5am woke up at 11:30. felt like shit. Ate cereal, did an ish, "missed" did another. Feel ok. Meeting lawyer in a couple hours, just plugged up toilet. Dope sure does help my guts, haven't had much diareha since I started. Well just wanted to check in & make sure you're going to be with me today, love you…(drawn happy face)

9:45pm. Well everything turned out pretty good! Bruce doesn't think we'll have any problems. As long as you are with me. Talked to Jess and Val & young James is supposed to bring some weed by tomorrow. Did my last ish about 6pm (I thought it was the big one) tweaked on stupid shit for a minute then got the munchies. Called Chip. It doesn't look like anything is going to happen tonight. Full stomach. I guess I'll be going to sleep early tonight, probably wake up sick tomorrow. Oh well. I sure do miss Marissa! Well I'm gonna finish my beer & crash. If I don't write tomorrow you'll know why. But I'll talk to you. I love you & thanks for being there for me today, goodnight…

FRIDAY 13 2:10pm woke up at noon, sick. Chip came right over to remedy that, told him he's a life saver, is he?

4/14 7:30 Hi, excuse the mess, learning how to refill the ink in my pen, don't know if it's going to work? Anyway yesterday Joy called & wanted a couple of rigs, I told her it would cost her a ride to pick up prescriptions, she comes over with a total butch lesbian named Tamica. They offer to get me high, so we do a little dope, I'm assuming this is Joy's new s/o? (what ever works?) they take me to primary, get scripts. (I'm sitting in back mind you & they take me right back home, worked out great but before I left Sue called & said she was going to pick up Marissa but had to run a lot of errands & she would call when she got back, so I'm just chillin not really tweaking & Teri just shows up. We kick it for a while. She asks if Chip is coming by. I didn't want to tell her he already had but we talked about it & she tells me she wants some but she doesn't want me to do any. In other words she doesn't want to share, so I say whatever & call Chip. After a while,

I bust out my stash & split it in ½ put a boulder in the spoon. Bell ringer! So we were waiting for Sue & Chip & I call Sue, she's home w/ Marissa she says she's grumpy and she's going to keep her for a few days. Sue tells me this she doesn't ask. I ask if I can come see her, Sue says she has to rescue and iguana and she'll call me when she gets back maybe later or tomorrow. I hang up the phone, trippin, she's taking my Iguana from me? I've been trippin hard on it all night and she never called back last night. Here it is 8am the next day I slept 1 hour, feel kinda shitty tomorrow's Easter I didn't even send Jess a card. (which I have) got to pay Ed's storage today & don't know if Teri will feel up to it, anyway things look pretty bleak right now so I'm going to do a little prayer & meditation. I'll talk to you soon. Love...

11:04am. Very bad reaction ...cotton fever...I think...bad trip...did another small shot feel a little better. Consequences. Still Shakey...

5:50pm Guess what? Paid Ed's storage for this month & MARISS'A HOME!!! Poor things skin & bones & walking real high, but she's home and I think very happy to be here. It's going to be a rough month but worth it. Teri & I impressed Sue with our iguana handling abilities, (feeding her by tube) oh by the way, thank you very very much, I knew you were listening. Love always & forever.

4/15 3:20am Happy Easter Jesus! (drawn happy face) 1:50pm I believe Easter is the day you were resericted , am I right? I had a bizarre typical conversation with Joy this am. Almost told her to come over. I feel very thrashed right now. Tweaked all night. Have to call Jess. Happy Easter. Marissa's still resting. She looks miserable. Must go and rest now or something. Bye.

4/15 Tax day! 6pm slept until 1pm felt good! Woke up, did small ish, felt good. Two things that made Easter Ok yesterday were talking to Jess and Chip coming by w/ Easter dinner, had leftovers for breakfast, Schauntell came by & Sue took Marissa to vet for shots. Turns out she has worms. Got medicine, house clean, everything real

The Bottom is Six Feet Under

mellow & relaxed. Chip & Lance coming by. I assume for an issue. I hope I feel this calm Thursday! So everything is cool. Don't have any chaos to report at present, but I'm supposed to call Joy so I'll keep you posted...bye...

4/19 4am – Hi, sorry I haven't written, came down, had section 8 inspection, Marissa spent night at Sue's. Chip said he scored that night. Was supposed to come by. 10:30 he called, we decided he would come by before work. We were both burnt. He didn't show until 2pm w/ Sean in rollerblades. He said he had the kind !! Pure. He made 3 issues, did mine, got rid of the sickness, felt a little better, they leave, I vacuum & lay down on couch. Fall asleep, wake up 2 hours later w/ munchies. Chip & Sean show back up and he does up 3 big ones. I did all of mine & cough. That one worked!! Teri comes over, so Chips got to turn diamond into cop today, good luck! Ok... Enough dope talk. Kinda. Well today eight hours from now I'm due for my SSI hearing & what am I doing up at 4:30am? I'm having complete faith in you and the judge. I could write a lot more but I'm going to slam a few beers and try to crash. Clean comforter. I feel pretty good now. I really think things are going to be good. I love you . Bye. (drawn happy face).

7pm Hi, well, full benefits, all done, except to wait & paper work. No more exams, lawyers, judges, etc. I got it. A landslide decision. Still in shock. Wow! Thank you Jesus! I did feel you the whole time! Now I get to call Val and ask when I can have Jess. My life is going to change. Drastically. I still can't believe the events leading up to and during the hearing. Do some killer dope last night crashed a 5am. Chip called at 8:30am comes over, we do an ish, he doesn't know what to do about the diamond. I asked him if the word prison means anything to him, I think he's setting himself up. & of course, I do another ish before I got to the hearing, that's when you let me know you were still here. A lot of prayers and a lot of faith payed off!! Teri is a mess! I've never seen her in so much pain before, I'm kinda glad she didn't make it to the hearing, afterwards went to pick up script for percodan. Back home to meet Sue for Marissa's vet appointment. Chip back by w/ Billy, going to have to talk to him about that, I like Billy but don't trust him at all, everybody doing issues & Schauntell shows up. I let her in Chip & Billy come out of my room Chip spinning. Me looking very guilty. She knew what she was doing. So anyway, just fed Marissa. Projects all put away and I'm completely burnt out! Can hardly think straight a lot of shit for a disabled guy. What a trip. So I'll talk to you soon…bye…

 4/22 9:18am Can't remember the last time I slept was I'm pretty sure I'll just drop pretty soon. Me, Chip, Billy & Lance slammin a lot! Of good dope (bell ringers a lot!) trippy, usually when I don't write it's because I'm drying up, just the opposite, I'm so thrashed I cant write anymore. Important stuff today. Cute vet tech coming over to give Marissa a shot. Told Teri I might come over and work? Plant fell on desk last night. Freaked me the fuck out! Spent the rest of the night cleaning up the mess. Pat came by yesterday brought hat rack, table, tackle box. 12:10 ok. Got a 1 hr power nap. Cleaned up plant mess. Pot pie in oven. I really wish these thumbs would heal. They hurt like hell! Don't know when vet tech is going to come by. I told Teri if se wanted me to help her today she had to call me. She hasn't yet. Oh well. Feeling much better, haven't prayed to you lately, I'm sorry I've been very spun. But you are always in my heart! (drawn happy face) Haven't done any dope yet did I mention that? Bye. Not much left to tweak on here. Hopefully Chip will be here by 4 and wake me up & I can go to Teri's if I feel up to it & work. She's being kinda a bitch but I can deal with it…don't know if vet tech will be here today or tomorrow? I think I kinda like her, she's not that good looking but I really liked her personality. Unfortunately she's married to a guy who has 2 degrees (college) and refuses to get a real job. Beautiful day! Perfect weather. Thank you Jesus!! I love you!

 4/23 4:50am Not very awake, though, comfy in my bed, a couple of beers & pipe hits. Might have to go work for Teri. Marissa had a bad day yesterday. Force feeding her and having to wrestle her to do it. & then Sue comes over & gives her her shot. She really freaked out then. Gonna crash. Goodnight… <u>DON'T FORGET TO CALL JESS AT 1:00 HER TIME ABOUT JASON, CALL ANN & DDS. SEE YA!</u>

4/23 1:05pm Pen tweak last night. Can you tell? (Words are all in bold calligraphy). Nice pens. Terrible heartbearn. Passed out at 4am. Tom called at 7am. Hinted about tweakin. Went back to sleep woke up at 11:30 dope hangover. Ate a little had a real hard time hitting myself w/ last ish. Called Teri, she's not up yet. Schauntel called & I had a real bad attitude. She wants me to come & do her laundry. This damn heart burn is tearing me up. Well I guess I should start the day, it is a beautiful day! I love you Jesus! (drawn happy face)

7:10pm waiting impatiently for Chip, always waiting, I am at his mercy. He leaves me just enough to keep from getting sick, but not enough to get me high. I think sooner or later he's going to get busted. I don't wish that on anyone, but I think in my case it would be the best. Except of course, if I'm with him. Did my little ½ ish I had left, tasted it with 7 units of med, took the sick away. Found a new spot to hit. No Teri's again today. Talked to Jess at one today, she sure is excited about this summer. I need to call Bruce tomorrow. Thank him and find out if its' 77% positive + Chip just called, he'll be here in 15.

1:18am Chip & Lance came by, did an ish took me to the 7-11. left a little dope for me & Teri. Wants to get rigs tomorrow. Sean calls, wants to know if him & his fiancé, who just got out of prison, & I won't even say how she "got out"…could stay the night. What could I say? The last 2 doses had made me sick, so I was just going to crash, they get here, Chip says everything's ok. We're going to bedroom to get high & I go to put Marissa in her tank…I put her on the ground for a minute…Sean for a big boy is scared to death of her, all of the sudden, I hear Marissa take off flying across the room, I don't know if she sensed his fear, all the stress she's had or what, but I have NEVER seen her (or Sean) move like that before. So it's (illegible) & I'm going to try to crash, I don't think I'll have any trouble getting to sleep. Only you know what will happen tomorrow. I will try to write, if not I will talk to you. Goodnight. Please protect me & my house, Marissa and Jessica. I love you Jesus! Thank you. (drawn happy face).

4/24 1:05pm I survived the slumber party. Got a good night's sleep. Chip came at lunch & picked them up. I split my dope with Sean and Chip didn't have any when he got them so looks like I'm gonna be a little sick this afternoon. (What else is new)? Well, I better start doing something. Marissa ate a whole salad this today! (drawn happy face) love you!!

Another nothing day. Nothing accomplished! I didn't even call Bruce. Can't let myself drift into negativity. Well I better give Marissa her medicine and I'll try to think positive! See ya!

4/25 2:15am Couldn't get wired all day. Don't know if it was the dope or me. Tired & hungry all day. Have not had any since 4pm & still felt dope sick all day. Spins, head rushes, etc. Did a little cleaning at Teri's (very little) might go back over tomorrow. Doubt it unless Chip comes by at lunch. Doubt that too. Must be realistic! God I wish I could just stop, and keep feeling the way I do right now. Anyway I need to make a small list, I'm not tweakin, and don't be surprised if I don't write for a little while…it's probably a good sign. Goodnight.

8pm Well sure enough, just when I decide to go the long haul, Chip calls. He came by to get me & called from downstairs & was too sick to come up & get me. Then go back down to get rigs at rx. I told him I was too sick to come down but I did it. So me, Chip & Lance make it to Walgreens & got generic needles. Came home and did a bell ringer, gibbered on for a while w/ Lance he said he's going back to recovery home. Good for him! I'm jealous. Got 2 issues left they might be back? Oh well, I'm fine now. Marissa pooped today! YEA! She's really getting back to her old self.

4/27 11:24am Chip & Lance came over & woke me up at 8 am. I'm going to bring myself down, I don't think Chip wants to make an extra trip every day to give me free dope, so I'm going to try hard not to call him. Very shitty day yesterday. Rode bike to Teri's, had to lay down for a while. I think I was reacting to bad dope. Katrina came by. (What a cutie). I guess I'm going to Teri's again. Nice day for a

The Bottom is Six Feet Under

ride. Oh, I had a message from Eduardo, saying I'm off the hook! Cause Chips been coming over all the time & that we gotta have a talk. So that makes my bad day even worse. I'll bet you can't guess who told him? Joy, big surprise! So she calls, tells a few lies & tries to change the subject by telling me she snitched on Chip & everybody in that circle. I think it's more BS. I do think she turned Billy & Ashley in. (Cops looking for Billy at Stacy's now). But it's definitely time to start making some changes in my lifestyle. Anyway, feel pretty good today, beautiful day. I love you Jesus! Thanks! Talk to you soon (drawn happy face).

4/28 12:39am – Teri's sitting here talking my ears off! Not a very good day. Got to Teri's and had to rest for a while. Couldn't get a whole lot done. Too many headrushes. Took a power nap & ate some ribs, felt a little better. Very small issue I practically had to beat out of Teri. Still didn't feel well. Maybe you're reminding me that I have a disability. Well I accept it. I told her we would get <u>all</u> of her chores done. <u>ALL.</u> Chip came by Teri got another ½, hopefully it will work for me this time. Anyway, it's late & I feel pretty fair. I thank you for the way I feel right now. I'm just going to say this once to you, I'm going to try and quit dope around the 7th of May. & try not to call Chip. He'll probably call me & I'm sure I will do the dope before the 7th, I just can't dry up without food. Really need to prepare for this one! I know you're with me & that's the biggest help! So I'm gonna give it a try. So that's about it for now. Chip also dropped off the headlight for the bike. $150 headlight. (Sweet). Talk to you soon. (drawn happy face).

4/29 8:11 am – No sleep yet. Yesterday Chip comes over to take me to Teri's 2 pick up money. I get there and of course she's talking poor Janette's ear off a mile a minute & I'm needing an ish pretty badly. So we finally leave to take Janette home & do some dope at my pad & right away she starts in about how I said I was going to buy the whole MGB? I don't know where she comes up with this shit. & then she's dishin out the CR puts a little tiny bit of stuff in spoon pours out about a $30 rock for herself. We argue about it for a while & I go about my business. Get pretty wired but not enough to put up w/ her *talk talk talk about the same shit over and over again & again. She jumps my case worst than Dad did for usually something that was her fault, all that shit she said she had to change about me. It's her. All my bad habits she's got far worse than me. So we get back to her pad and I just start in on the patio. I spent + - 3 hours in spider webs & rabbit shit checking to see if I'm still doing what she wanted. It was a nightmare! By 9pm I'm so dope starved (she's not though) tired & hungry. I'm ready to just escape, run out this front door & don't look back. I just don't know what happened to us. Was it the dope? Am I really a jerk? I don't think so. I just can't stand to be around her, especially spun. And I'm SICK of my house smelling like cigarette smoke! Oh well. Only time will tell. But I've got at least 2 more days of this abuse. Hopefully today she'll be on morphine & out all day! Oh yea! & last night I get home & Chip calls says nothing going tonight. I've got I've 1 ish left, walk up to the store, get back home sick. Hunger pains, nausea, fatigue, just plain exhausted. So I'm trying to decide weather to do last ish & try to cut the mirror to fit in the frame & Teri actually found the glass cutter I'd been asking for for weeks. I'm nodding, phone rings, it's Lance. The Eagle has landed. They will be here in 15. I really don't feel like doing any now so they get here, Chip looks like I feel. He says what do you need, I said food. Just so happens he's got healthy cereal & milk in the car, so we all sat down, watched TV & ate cereal before we did our issues. It turned out to be weak dope, I felt it but what I did should have spun me. Lance feels real bad. (I think Lance & Chip are lovers?) But anyway, I do feel better. They work out another deal (keep in mind there's is only to hold them over until shipment comes tomorrow) do they go to get more & I tweak out on the mirror. Fucking it up naturally, so instead of having one big mirror, I have many small mirrors. Multitasking at it's best. To make a long story short they come back, we got spun. They left I made a mess in my bedroom & stayed up all night, hurt like hell. So that's it for now. I love you Jesus, Bye (drawn happy face)*

9:00pm – Hello, feeling a bit tired but other than that, no complaints, had kinda a rough day, cleaned the whole house, had a stereo war w/ downstairs neighbor. Saw Katrina (last visit) talked for about an hour. I think I was a bit sketchy at times, oh well she's married & I'm disabled & impotent. Spent some quality time w/ Marissa. Called Teri, she said I woke her up but she talked my ear of until I just about hung up on her. Now she has the Joy effect on me (bums my high out) Chip called said he'd be here in 3 hrs. I'm needin some dope bad. Oh well, so he shows up on time w/ groceries. Can you believe that? What a guy. Lance due to go back to rehab tomorrow. I'll be weird to see Chip without him. Also talked to Ed today for a while he's doing good. Chip also brought 7 new CD's. (YEA)! Tomorrow's Teri's surgery. Sitting in the waiting room for 2 + hours. I'll probably be nodding. I hope she saved some dope. (Doubt it)! Oh well, I feel like riding over there but something's telling me not to. So I'm going to listen to me. Anyway, everything's cool right now. Praise You! I love you Jesus! Thanks! (drawn happy face)...

4/30 10:20am – *Crashed early last night slept like a rock. Woke up feeling good! Thank you Jesus! Maybe I feel so good because I was praying when I fell asleep? Whatever the reason, thank you. Please be with Teri today & let this procedure be a success. Love (drawn happy face).*

4:45pm – *I survived! Dropped Teri off at UCDMC & went to pick up rigs. Went back to UC & had a positive talk with Teri. Long wait a little sleep, not very comfortable, 3 hours & Teri comes out her old self went home & made had some food & Teri kicked almost a whole issue! Wow! So we're sittin here, she's babbling, pretty mellow, Chip on his way. Then to Teri's to do a little work $$ talk to you later, thank you, I'm sure Teri thanks you too!*

5/1 11:15am – *Long talk w/ Teri about getting sober. Also had the talk w/ Chip. Me & Teri's talk ended up both of us frustrated and unable to get our points across. So she took me to get my bike at 1:00am I rode home. (nice ride) & called her & we had a good talk. When Chip came over by last night, he didn't look too good. We did a large ish of mystery dope? It wasn't great. But when Chip was leaving I asked if he would leave me some. He left a very large sack! But anyway, I ended up staying up until 8am. Today doing nothing.*

Not much left to tweak on here. <u>That's good though</u>. Still shootin for the 7th or 8th. Must think positive! I do have SSI coming. Jess' b-day on the 21st. must do something for her! Beautiful day! But maybe a little to windy for bike ride. Well, I'm going to call Chip & remind he to call investigators about diamond. Bye…

1:25pm yesterday, when Teri came to get me I had Ravi playing when the doctors asked if she wanted some music the jokingly told her, sorry we don't have any Ravi Shankur! Sign. Just chillin so far today. I've got kinda upset stomach. See ya…

1:05 am Hi. I haven't done a lot of dope today, puked a little, ate a lot. I must have a screw loose, but I invited Joy over for an ish. I'm lonely. Probably gonna get pictures from Rite Aid, for Jess. Chip & I have been talking A LOT about recovery. He knows where I stand & my due date. I feel almost like I'm pressuring him into doing it (if anybody is, it's Lance). I am so ready to do an ish. I just hope I don't blow chunks.

5/2 5:35pm Well it turned out to be quite and interesting evening last night, Joy got there, looking better than I've seen in a while… did a couple of bellringers, started talking…first mistake. She gets all serious & says she wants me to apologize for being the first to hit her. That made me VERY ANGRY! One thing lead to another, heated discussion about recovery, Chip & the gang, cops, Rio Linda, etc. Finally we agree to take a shower & fool around, the whole time she was talking about snitches, getting busted, etc. & I'm getting a little paranoid. We made it into the shower about an hour or two later really in the mood (excited) afterwards we jump in bed naked. All of the sudden we start arguing again. She puts her pants on. The whole thing is about Chris rattin on Chip & I want to warn Chip…and stay out of trouble myself. I just didn't know if she was lying or not.

6:30 am and I'm in the kitchen eating Vienna sausages & she comes out laughing & says she was just fucking with my head the

The Bottom is Six Feet Under

whole time... I Lost it! First I pointed to the front door & said GO! She got all surprised. Wait I need to shower later...

5/3 3:40am – Hello, I guess I can try to pick up where I left off gotta fly though. Bedtime and vision almost gone completely. So I tell her to GO! I haven't any idea what happened. I just lost it, & I *now* really don't think she meant any harm judging from her surprise. But I just snapped, I wonder if it's because that's the kinda thing she used to do to me? But it definitely pushed buttons that haven't been pushed in a long time. I followed her into the bedroom so she could get her stuff (and none of mine, which reminds me, she seems sure she snagged some of Teri's pens from Billy and gave them to her friends) if I had proof, I would make a very big deal over it, but I have no proof. & I get the impression that she wants something for the effort. Go figure. All I know is, if Teri asks for them back, she's going to be Very Upset!!! & if I didn't look like a big enough fool, I even gave Billy one of the *very few* remaining pens. Well, you live & learn. Back to Joy... She takes back everything the kids gave me, school pictures, cross, etc & I just want her out! My temper is rising by the second, somehow I spilled my last bit all over the desk (big mess) somehow I manage to heard her toward the front door, still getting madder and madder, & she turns around and says "You better not hit me", I say just GO! I told her I wasn't going to hit her, but it's been many years since I felt that kind of rage! Thank you Jesus for not letting me do something real stupid. & she left. I did feel very relieved when she left, but the situation left me in a funk. Bummed my high out. And I was kinda waiting for the police to roll up on me & I couldn't take the stress. I have to crash now. (illegible) nodding vision almost gone. Goodnight.

12:09pm Man, did I need that sleep! Calve cramp brought me out of deep sleep & bed quick! Felt very sick! Ate some, felt a lot better. Bells are ringing too so, to finish the Joy thing, she left & I got paranoid because I divulged some info about Chip I probably shouldn't have, so I called her to apologize. & since then she's still callin. The end of that one. Chip came by last night and I had been tweakin hard for like 24 hrs we went & picked up my pictures. $13 but worth it. Got some neat stuff out of dollar bins (tools etc) then to Costco. Return shirt finally. & had some dinner. Constantly trying to prepare myself for the 8th. Gotta run, talk to you later...

5/4 5:38am – Good morning! Just about bed time, talked to Jess tonight, she's got a very bad cold. Hope she's better real soon! 4 days & counting until D day. Still preparing self & home. I'm going to miss Chip, but not the rest of the crowd. I should make a list of tweak priorities for these last few days. Schauntell came by brought some homemade Chicken soup. Boy, I'll tell ya, for a guy as messed up as I am, I sure do have a lot to be grateful for! But I really need to get out of this rut. I have faith that once I get a decent car, things will change drastically! Well, I better sleep now. Good night. (drawn happy face).

5:40pm Chip came by woke me up, well, did a total bell ringer! Spun hard! Then got tired? Don called, good to hear from him! Need to get motivated. Change is going to be good! Latter!...

8 pm Not feeling well. I'm sure all this dope & tweakin is taking a real toll on my body, as well as my mind and spirit. But I have faith & I know you'll be with me the whole time. (drawn happy face) I guess I'll make some Top Ramen & see if that makes me feel any better. Talk to you soon...

5/5 4:09am if someone who doesn't know me was reading this journal they would think I kept some pretty strange hours. Just wanted to check in. Nothing exciting going on spent entirely too much time rebuilding fan in my room (multitasking) going to crash soon. See ya...

8:10 pm Hi. Interesting day. Passed out at 7 am woke up at 8:30am wide awake. Felt like I slept for hours. Did a few a tweaky projects, Chip came by we got spun & just kinda hung out, it was pretty cool. Both of us kinda reluctant to stick that needle in our arms, after quite a while I went for it, got it on the first time, don't do that much anymore. Everything is ok. Billy & Ashley came by for some hustle. I confronted Billy about it, he denied it, & said it was probably Dan. I believe him. I don't even know if I am missing any? Oh well, after the 9th I doubt I'll ever see them again. Plus the thought of going to Target w/ stolen checks scares me but being broke & out of so many things makes it sound really cool. Please God, don't ever let me go there again. Please, in Jesus name, let the rest of my life be filled with peace, love and happiness. Just called Chip, he still hasn't left his house yet. He's bringing his PlayStation, that's cool with me. I sure do hope he quits the "D". ok. And Joy called for some things. I guess I'll give her some. Have to. But I'm going to leave them somewhere she can pick them up and I don't have to see her. Gonna run now bye…

5/6 5:15am – Chip finally shows up at 9:30 target closes at 10 we rush over there, Chip doesn't see any p station 2 games he likes, says I can get some stuff, we're flying through the store, Chips little legs givin mine a run for the money. I got a few things I HAD to have. Thank you Jesus & Chip! I found out some serious crimes Chip has been committing, I better not write them down. I've felt like I was very stoned for the past few days. (BAD) I think it's lack of sleep also seeing things that aren't there & not seeing things that are. Double & Triple vision. Having a very difficult time writing as you can see, (barely legible), so we get back from Target, my heads spinnin, Chip gets me some Rolaids. TY again. Chip tells me to go eat & he'll make up the issues. 1st he starts to hook up the PlayStation & breaks (hopefully fixable) my VCR & then realized he left the dope at home. I thought I was the only one that far out there. Billy comes over for Chips last 3. Today throwin darts in my room I could smell Billy here. Smelled like a lot of slammed dope comin out in sweat and no shower for quite a while, mixed up that smells like death. So since he left, I've been disinfecting the whole house! Joy told me Billy only has 1 ball and can't get an erection. And that mixed with the death smell & the chicks love him? OK. I can't write anymore. Tired. Cant see. Goodnight.

10am Got maybe 2 hours sleep. Feel pretty hung over or run over. Chip was supposed to call before 10 and we were going to wrecking yard. No word from him yet. Ok, well, no biggie, was going to try to

Valerie Covert

go back to sleep. Neighbors behind me mowing big lawn, so scratch that idea, need more sleep desperately. 3 days left. HELP.

    1:50pm No more sleep. Had an old issue of mystery dope left. Did it & it pissed me off. Made eggs & ham, Sam I Am, didn't eat much. Marissa had a big breakfast and she's got to be ready to poop soon! She still doesn't look very well, doesn't' move much. I'm really starting to feel come-downish and VERY VERY angry! Don't know why? 5 Car loads of Mexicans outside my window having a fiesta. Blocking my parking space & my peace of mind. I can't wait until I don't have to come down any more, but the last one is going to be the B.

    5/7 12:20pm – Hi. Got a few hours of sleep this morning. Chip called & woke me up. I think I sounded a lot worse than I felt, didn't feel good though, d-sick. So I told him don't trip, I'm cool. He was gonna come by at lunch w/ fast food & ish. I said OK. Little Chinese Jehovah Witness lady cam by. Feeling NEGATIVITY surging through my veins, heart & brain. Like a fat bellringer. Anxieties, things I haven't felt since the beginning of this lesson. Also very sketchy. Have to keep myself in check. (am I just paranoid)? Can't get ahold of Teri. Is she avoiding me? I've got way too much to do to make my decent as painless as possible. I've noticed, somewhere along the line, I started concentrating on Chip & my little sculpture in there than remembering to stop & smell the flowers and thank Jesus for giving them to us. Temp. crown is starting to hurt. My lesson for that bag was they dropped me like a bad habbit. Left with a piece of shit in my mouth that's probably going to fall apart. Am I thinking positive? Check yourself! Chip brings KFC, BBQ sloppy Joe thing, I can't stand those when they're made good, this one was bad. I wolfed it down, big ish, flyin!

    5/8 1pm – Yesterday was a trip! Chip came over after work. HOT outside! Picked up food stamps and went to Fry's. A few head rushes but all things considered I was feeling quite a lot better than expected. Then home for some AC & ish. Then to Target spun Chip & I can't decide on cereal for Lance. Then to drop off groceries. I was a little *more spun than I wanted to be when I saw Lance (at rehab) but, everything was cool. (good to see Lance) Before all of this I talked to Schauntell, she was more depressed than I have EVER seen her! & she needed me Bad! I could just not be there for her. I told her I was going to get spun and she started crying, begging me not to, I guess she doesn't remember what it was like out here. Where you have to inject poison into your veins EVERYDAY just to ALMOST function as a human. She also had a run-in with a neighbor. The neighbor punched her in the face, etc. Bad trip for her. I can feel her pain, something I have been able to do sometimes (sympathy pains) she said she quit praying, does that sound like Schauntell? So wouldn't you know it, I flaked on her, but I asked Teri to talk to her & I think she did. I called her at 9:30pm. Me & Chip were in West Sac, I don't even know what we were doing or where we were, just tweakin. I know Chips getting low on dope & I ran the risk of running out for the night, I wasn't trippin though. He suggested that I just wait until he runs out to quit. I'm not gonna sweat the small shit! Everyone knows my pattern. I say I'm gonna quit on the 9th It'll be at least the 11th. So on the way home Justin (tonight's connect) pulls up next to us on freeway & calls Chip, how's that for timing? I was just going w/ it. Enjoying the co. & the high. Stopped & talked for a minute, came home did a sm. Ish & Chip left. I told him don't worry about leaving any. I'm sure somewhere around here there's an ish. He left, I ate…a few minutes went by Chip calls & asks if they can do a deal here. I said ok. Knowing this is all ending soon, plus I've wanted to meet Justin and Rosalin for a while. So they get here, they're the most normal working ones in the gang. A lot of dope in my house, a stolen U-haul van in my spot, 1 diabetic, 1 ex-con – that dresses like Ward Cleaver & goes to work everyday as an accountant, but can shoot dope like the rest of us. 2 Fugitives that are wanted all over the country. Wouldn't you know it, it's 12:01am – tomorrow, the 8th. D Day. But I wasn't' paying attention & Chip told J to kick hard. He did. The one time I cared if I didn't get any he throws me a Boulder of the SCREAM! J says & knows it's a gnarly kick & I'm thinking yes, but it's nowhere near worth losing everything I have over, so they all left. I thought about crashing & didn't until 7:30am. Mellow day today so far, thank you Jesus! I must still be gibbering. Oh well, talk to you later… (drawn happy face)*

5/9 4:40am – Too much to write after a couple of pipe hits. Needless to say, I didn't quit yet. I am, without a doubt, a true junkie. In every sense of the word. Did junkie stuff all day, passed out and came too w/ very very bad insulin reaction. I gotta crash now. Bye...

4:40pm – Weird! As careful as I was not to forget Schauntells B-day, I did. But I did manage to get up & give Teri a wake up call and take her to Dr.'s apt & pick up test strips, pay Ed's storage. It's VERY hot out. Sick. Must go now. Talk to you soon.

8:45pm Sweatin like a hog in the bathroom! Chip came by after work, said his niece wants to buy the bike for $500. Bummer!. But if it's true I sure as hell would jump on it if I was him, but I can't help to wonder if he's not ready to give up the dope. He knows I can't be around him if he's still doing it, maybe he's trying to play it safe, or maybe he's sketchin on me. Who knows? I'm not going to trip on it. Just keep my eyes open & watch for signs & TRY to stay positive. See ya! (drawn happy face)

5/10 6:00am – Hi, for some reason, I've got this feeling this is one of the last sunrises I'm going to see for a long time? Either way, I'm not going to stress. Joy came by, picked up a couple of the generic rigs & some Vicodin. Brought a 6 pack of Coors Light. Can you believe that? I told her to leave me alone! We'll see if she does. Goodnight.

7:45pm I must tell you about some feelings I'm having right now. If feel inside that the time has come for this insanity to end, but, with that, an even worse insanity takes over, the dry up. And of course I'm not prepared. So if it is indeed my time I'm just going to rely on you God, if anything will get me through this it's you. I am afraid. I don't know why. It's pretty scary being addicted to drugs. I can't do <u>anything</u> unless I'm high. Not even get out of bed. It comes before anything! Help me God. Please!!

11:35 No dope. Feel good though, hungry. Talked to Val & Jess tonight. Val and I talked a lot. Sometimes I really Miss, Love & Adore that girl. Not a day goes by that I don't think about all of this I guess I just stuff it. So I plan on telling Mom tomorrow that Jess is coming out this summer & her & Lanne are more than welcome to come here & visit her, but she's not going there. I'm pretty sure Mom will think it's revenge or something, but that's her stuff. I feel you already helping to make this into a positive or at least not make it so negative. Which at one time, I would have lost it, but now I just want the truth.

5/11 12:40pm – Scraped my last bag. Woke up a little, following Marissa around hoping she will poop, for Vet. Talked to Teri, felt better about situation, just need to process & wait. Don't know what's going on with Chip? I'm not going to trip though. In fact, I'm not going to stress at all! I may not feel very good in a few hours, who knows? I do know I will survive. The only things that have me worried are the heat making me pass out at Vet's office and disappointing Teri by not working today. Play it by ear. Chip called, on his way, for lunch. I don't know if it's worth it to talk to him about respect & honesty or if even…I don't know, maybe it's all me? No biggie. I will survive! See ya!

1:45pm – Chip just left. I was sketchin I think. He looks sober and sincere. Brought burgers & asprin? I don't know what I'm trippin on. I feel ok right now. Sue called. I told her the heat tears me up. She said we'll use the AC & stop at Baskin Robins. Cool! I am bothered by the fact that I made some plans for later that I know I won't be able to keep, if I'm waiting for dope & if I have the dope, chances are I'll be extremely spun. Don called & I told him to come over after work. I really miss him, but at this point I'll I don't know. Need to think positive! That's all!!!

10:43pm – Well, all's well that ends well, of course the day went a lot smoother than antisapated, except for Vet appointment. I looked real bad, dripping with sweat, very dizzy. I wonder what Katrina thought? She's the first girl I've thought about being with in a long time! I just think she would be fun to be with. Sue said she would way rather see her w/ me than her husband. I told her I don't think I could give her what she deserves. Oh well. Came home & ate and then crashed. Had a few phone calls, don't remember what I said. Teri came to get swamp cooler at 9:00am. I woke up to make something to eat. Called Chip. On his way over w/ ½ gram of Bills. We had Chicken Pies & veggies & lg. issues, not great. Mixed a little mystery in & it works. He left me with a couple to get through the night. I think he is straight up? Talk to you later. Can't stop sweating... (drawn – small – happy face).

    5/12 10:15pm – Mom and Lanne had Frank put to sleep today. Rest in peace Frank...Slept until 6am. Chip picked me up and we went to Dave's to meet Justin & Roslynn. Did fat issues, spun hard, didn't get wired though. Came home, Chip left and ish & scraper bag. Did another ish and ½. Now I feel it. Chip was supposed to come back. I doubt if he will. Oh well, beggers can't be choosers. Bye.

    5/13 12:25 am Well I'm wired but not spun. I guess it's the whole first day thing. Looks like I'll be alone too. Don't feel like tweakin. (nothing really to tweak on). I guess I should just crash. Talked to Jess. (drawn happy face). Can't wait to see her. Today Joy called & left message that David & Kyle found syringe in Kyles CD case (probably Billy's) wants me to tell them it was mine, get her out of this jam. <u>Nothing</u> she does surprises me. So when she calls, I'm going to tell her never to call again & if she does I'll just have to change my #. (I <u>really</u> don't want to). & I'm sure she'll slander me anyway to David & Kyle. God bless them. Well, I guess I'll go to bed now. Good night. (drawn happy face)...

    4:45am. Chip went back to Davis, got some new stuff, came by, very large issue. Nothing. More garbage. Neither of us could keep our eyes open. Shit happens. Joy called a couple of times. I wish she would stop! Goodnight...again...

10:41am – Mother's Day. Woke up with intense crank hangover. Had some cereal, Chip left a good size ish of some bunk stuff. I did ½ of it and spun for a while…? Maybe we both missed last night? Think I'll give him a call. Talk to you later.

8:26pm – Not too bad of a day. Did an issue of some almost real dope, went to Target w/ Chip then he drops me off w/ an ish of garbage. Said he would bring a doggie bag from Uncles, I doubt he'll be back tonight. Oh well, ya play, ya pay! Talked to Sue, she thinks Adam is sick. God be with him. I really hate being a junkie! Teri is doing a lot better. I had forgotten how cool she can be when she's not hurting. I had to lie to her…or…stretch the truth rather, I gave her the special crucifix that I made, the oak one. I think she liked it. I hope she does. I'm I'm wanting a fix <u>real</u> bad! But I think if I just keep going like this I could make up the lost sleep & still function, yeah right. I imagine Chips going to get tired of carrying me sooner or later, I just don't know what to do. His intentions are good, but it's not working for me. But I've noticed the only time I go through this is when Chips broke or has bunk dope? Who knows. Better just go with it. Think positive!! Don't beat yourself up! And remember that you have a lot more to be thankful for than a whole lot of people!!! So deal with it & remember it's <u>mind over matter</u>, ok, I feel a little better. Talk to you later…

5/14 – 2:34am – No dope. Can hardly cope. Lowered myself to actually call Joy. I'm sure that made her feel good? Well guess I'll do dishes & eat something & sleep until Chip comes by with the life blood. I'm at his mercy. No, I take that back. Everything will be ok! This too shall pass. LOVE.

10:00pm – Slept all day. Chip came by at 6 with burgers and last issue. He had to hit me. Good rush. We went shopping, healthy food. Few phone calls, mellow. Love….

5/15 1:51pm – Woke up to an ish from Billy & Ashley. Ok. A lot of sand, had to have Billy hit me. I think I must have an ear infection or something, the dizziness & head rushes are too intense. & maybe it's me and not the dope. Chip's been getting wired off of it…?? I wish Billy & Ashley could be trusted because their really pretty cool. Except Ashley's always making eyes at me. Sometimes in front of Billy & so when ever they come over Billy's sketchin on Ashley? I guess it's just the way it's supposed to be. This should be blue ink? Can't tell. Well I hope I can stand long enough to shower & shave. Not enjoying the headrushes & not being able to get wired! Just have to deal with it. Love. (drawn happy face). Chip <u>finally</u> hit pay dirt. Juans stuff. He bought a lot, for us not to sell, I guess it wasn't me after all. I don't think he likes it much? We're talking about the 21st target date to quit. (Note from author: he doesn't mention if he realizes that the 21st is our daughters birthday) Who knows. It's easy to talk about after a bellringer. I'm having a lot of trouble hitting myself! Sore arms! Everyone and their bros calling me tonight…George..Cliff (problems w/ Sherrys berry)..Eduardo, etc. Target, milk, rigs, descent night too much chili today. Teri's bro relapsed last week, dryin up at Teris. I had a feeling. Man, my arms are fucked up! As soon as Chip's ready, so am I, I hope Lance plans on staying sober! I guess the bike is gone! I wish he would just take the fucking thing! It makes me really sad lookin at it everyday! Well, gotta call Jess. Talk to you soon (drawn happy face) Love…

5/16 4:48am – Finally got some good stuff but missed so much I didn't really get to feel it. Did tweak a little. Stayed up all night. Trying to crash now. Contemplating calling Chip & have him come by before wk. I think I might be pushing it? DON'T KNOW WHAT TO DO? I think if I can crash, he'll come over at lunch. I hope and I really hope he plans on quitting. SOON! Well, I'm gonna try to sleep. If I can't I'm sure I'll write some more. Goodnight (drawn face with no smile only a squiggly line for a mouth – like a distressed face). Love. 4:10pm – Yea, I have a very strong feeling this whole thing is winding down. Chip just called from Woodland. He took Lance to court. Getting increasingly more dope sick by the minute, have been praying for strength all day! Trying to do the whole house clean up, running out of steam quick! I wish I could just tough this one out! I'm already ½ way there. Chip just called won't be here until 6 or so, come

The Bottom is Six Feet Under

on Lance, do the right thing. I really need to be thinking of plan B, because counting on Chip & Lance to get you sober is just setting myself up for failure. Dope fiend mentality. Did I tell you Teri's brother relapsed. She has been babysitting. Kerrie from Mather called. She's trying to get an apartment here. That would be cool! Haven't given up on trying to get Marissa out today. But I sure have been avoiding Jessicas card & Pics..? ok. breaktime's over. Talk to you later. Thanks for listening. Love...dope sick everyday, just enough to keep me...6pm – looking at Jess' card and her song by Blind Melon comes on the radio. Tears? I need some answers! I'm ok though. House is spotless & blessed w/ sage. Positive energy restored. Got to live in the now! & right now I'm alive & have <u>a lot</u> to be thankful for. (drawn happy face)...real good things are going to happen soon...watch..bye.

5/17 1:28am – BG 240 I'm going to start recording BG, etc. Chip showed up, we did very large issues & both immediately felt much better, then he leaves, I don't know if he's getting sick of me or what? No biggie. I really do have to concentrate on being the Matthew that people admired & looked up to. Not this dope fiend. It seems to me that when I quit jonesing & got off my ass & started cleaning and praying for strength, I started feeling better & grounded. If fact, when Chip got here & asked if I slept, even I was amazed remembering that I had not slept. I felt fine. Wonder what that means? Teri came by brought some soup in trade for some Trazedone for her bro. I miss her, man, she was a bitch before this last procedure. I did some calculating & if I'm correct, the Gross back pay should be about $29,000. I figure I should net about at least $10,000 not bad huh? Can you imagine? OK see ya! (drawn happy face). Love 5:30am – BG 188, large bowl of honeycombs then goodnight. Love....BG 503. 22units R. boy, that's a little bit high, it won't be long now before I can get in my car and drive to my doctors office & not have to wait 6 hours to be seen. Imagine, up all night again, good dope, did a few cool things, hooked up the waterfall. (for serenity). Finally filled out Jess' card. Hope there's enough postage on it. Kinda tired now. Starting to get heartburn. No Rolaids. Shit! Feeling extremely mellow, sitting on that damn stool all night just doesn't work. My back is killing me, should take a Vicodin & I got a ton of em. Kinda a trip lookin at pictures last night some of them I looked way sucked up! Tore up! But Jess looks great in all of them. That's about it for now. Bye. Love. (drawn cross, heart, happy face, yin yang sign, peace sign..) Jesus is my savior. 2:26pm BG 154 – Zapped by the heat, finally called Chip & told him Marissa & I would be down in the sun. & Sue called & said she would be over w/ meds, etc. & to have Juleus w/ me, so I put the leash on Marissa & went down. Sat in sun for a while. Man. Went into front yard of neighbors, the gang of young Mexican kids came over crowding Mar. she seemed fine though. "A lot better than me" so she poops on the lawn, then starts eating grass, then weeds, then anything she can get in her mouth. Well, we got our 15 + min in the sun & I can't hang. I go to pick her up & she flips out trying to get away. Does a death roll w/ leash on. I hold her up high branch style, she even looks like she'd going to bite me. She jumps out of my hand, lands on concrete. I don't think it hurt her, but I think it woke her up. So I think she just got spooked. We'll just have to take it slow. Just now starting to feel better myself. Chip & I went to 7-11, on the way to the car, Mexicans working on cars, probably the Chiva connect. Black people, car port opposite he's either crack or weed. This place, last year was like a senior complex, quiet & clean & now there's graffiti on the street, Chip said, there's the Chiva, there's the crack & there's the crank all in separate sides of the court. I didn't even realize it, but I'm right in the middle of all of this crap, just because, Chip & are clean & respectable doesn't make me innocent. Billy, Justin & Ross seen bring stolen vehicles here. Major drug deals, felons in & out. Open your eyes Goofball!! Who knows? Time to eat…bye…don't trip though, I'm cool.

    5/19 12:45am As usual another typically unusual day in the life of a very unusual junkie. Got out of shower, Billy, Ash & Chip here, ish already waiting for me, Bellringer. Cough & eyes fluttering, now we're going to see Lance at rehab. Where's the logic in that? He wasn't there so we just cruz the old hood. "Los Robles" a lot of memories. I always remember the good ones, even though I'm SURE there are FAR more bad ones. Then to Dimple (Records) for incense, back home, the bike goes bye bye - (drawn tears). No it just wasn't meant to be, who knows? Not trippin, did trip on Chip leaving just one issue. He said he suggests I do maintenance. SSSKKEETTCH. Billy & Ash show up again, we go back up, Chip gives Billy a Bellringer, loads the pipe for Ash, does an ish, leaves me high & dry. Actually got a fat ish in the room, but? No biggie. Kinda trippin they're all peakin & tweakin talking spun gibberish a good opportunity to see how ridiculous you behave on it. Went grocery shopping, did ok, got some beer. Chip dropped me off & I called Joy let her come & get few Vicodin, I don't know why? It was cool though. She gave me a night stand only her and me on drugs would want, feel ok though, & talked to Chip for a long time. I think I will do the last ish, Chip is definitely <u>not</u> your normal tweaker. I really like him a lot! I think sober, I would like him even more. (NOT GAY) Talk to you later...

3 am BG 462 Did last ish, got really nauseous? Something always goes wrong w/ the last one. I should be sleeping right now! Oh well. I got a number from Joy of a Dr. who specializes in Drug & Alcohol treatment, she says he doesn't always charge a fee. Can't hurt to call him? Well, I'm ready to throw in the towel. Time clean up shop & lay down. Bye Love. JESUS IS MY SAVIOR ALSO, TRY TO GET OUT OF (something here is scratched out and unreadable).

12:00pm – well, George is on his way over, I'm comin down. Chip isn't coming over. So I'm ready. Whatever!

3:10pm – well lots of excitement, actually woke me up with a little, so not so concrete. Big plans were made & somehow I laying in bed w/ Marissa, nobody here, no drugs, except a lot of beer. Almost out of chew, but feeling very peaceful. Had a real good talk w/ Schauntell. George calling everybody from my phone book, trying to get laid. I gave him Joy's phone #. Short conversation. She said you got any money? He said a lot, she said I'm on my way & I gave him some condoms. I doubt if he took them, IDIOT! Oh well, kinda waiting for Scooby snack from Chip or Bellringers from Rio Linda (Joy & George). Don't know if either will materialize & to be honest, don't care, at this point, it'll be interesting to see how it turns out! I will keep you posted as it unfolds. Talk to you later, love...

Valerie Covert

    5/19 7pm – Very interesting! Well about 6pm last night, I was feeling ok. Chip calls, on his way. Knock on the door. Surprise it's Billy & Ash. They just dropped in, then Chip shows up, Bellringers, so we all tweak for a while. Chip has to run errands. Anymore I don't trip if he comes back or not. I guess B & A are just gonna kick it here. It's cool. Ash talking a little too much but good times feeling good. Me & Billy did a little dumpster divin got a stereo cabinet, just what I need! Bill got computer. Chip actually comes back w/ green bud & CD & <u>tool</u>, more issues. I'm starting to wonder about George? Joy must be putting out? Chip goes home about 11pm. B & A still here, George finally shows up (looks spun), sees Bill & Ash says he had to move his car, goes back down stairs, phone rings, has to be Joy. She wants to talk to Ashley. Chaos everywhere. She goes! Ashley says she wants to make amends, Billy starts to sketch hard. Very strange look in his eyes. I told him respect my space, no bullshit, I think that snapped him out of it (I have to tell, Billy gave me a book to give to Jess. Ash told me she was going to get me a gift card for her B-day. I doubt she will, but it's the simple fact that they're the first ones who actually acknowledge that my home is a shrine to my daughter. I'm touched. I just wish I could trust them more. I really do think after I confronted them about pens they respect me more). But, anyway, they left. I picked up a bit expecting George to come in any minute. He never did. I got into a project w/parts of stereo cabinet. Chip left me w/ 2 issues, tweaked out! On project for hours. Kinda wondering about G. He calls at about 3am says he's on his way. Don't hear from him again until 10am. He's sketched hard (Rose – illegible)? Been stuck at Joy's alone all night. Can't find my #, too sketched to drive. I feel bad! Trying to find him a ride. Chip says he'll (illegible) starting to nod on toilet. I'll finish later. Peace, love and happiness. (drawn peace sign, heart and happy face)

    2:58am Going 1000mph. nodded at 9am. Trippin. Finished sanding night stand, looks good! Cleaned up everything cool. Except, I'm thrashed! & it's <u>very hot</u>!!! Wish I had slept last pm. Oh well, there will be plenty of time for that! Eyes <u>really fucked up</u>! Just wanted to check in. time management skills at work! Talk to ya later, much love!

5/21 – *Happy b-day Jess & Carly! To many bizarre things happening to remember. Last night Justin & Rose left a lot of good dope for a place to do an ish. Split it w/ George, went to Chips. Ashley, jail, Macys. They found EVERYTHING!!! (Illegible...to do laundry & chores at 11pm. Had a strange evening, beautiful house, dark, hard for me to see & walk, Billy was makin fun of me. I got pissed off! & then I realized I liked it a lot more than people worrying about me. I truly wish more people would react like that. Did an ish at 11:45 Big. Billy wanted to do it. I let him. Tweaked through the garage a little. Chips room, small but nice. Trip finally seeing it. I told Chip I was going to do a fat one when I got home. He seems real worried. I'm sketchier than I've ever been, in my life. Sometimes it's kinda fun, when I got home George was trippin WASTED HARD! House had a really very <u>strange</u> energy. I ended up just laying down w/ Marissa & crashing. Phone rings at 4:30. it's Ash, talked for a bit, I didn't have any info. So she's gonna call back. I sure hope Chip talks w/ Bill. 5am Joy calls, wants to buy what I have left. I'm horny so I tell her to get over here now, George takes off. He's got dope. Hope he makes it home alright. He ended up stopping in Stockton and getting $20. so Joy gets there, the house is thrashed. We get high! Talk A LOT!, Real good talk, very constructive, almost had sex. It seems like she finally understands me. I feel the unconditional love again. One sign after another all morning. I'm worried about what Chips going to think. I forgot to tell you. I think Billy might be BI. When we were at Chips they put a porn in. a good one! & Billy asked me if I liked men. I sorta sketched. & told him I was A-sexual. We watched porno for a few minutes. Made me very uncomfortable. Asked them to turn it off, but I took it home with me. So, Joy left. I started getting my house in order. Found a few syringes of REAL mystery, got the house spotless & passed out in Dads chair. 2 hours later, phone wakes me up, didn't have any idea who it was, talked for a while before I asked who it was. LEA. She moved to my hood & I think has been doin dope? Everything is mellow now. Chip picked up Lance & he's supposed to grad. Julius payed me $20. all in all, a very productive day. THANK YOU JESUS. Lance really liked his cross. (drawn happy face) time to wind down, batt dying in phone & I <u>have</u> to call Jess. Write to you soon. Love!*

5/22 11am – Well, it looks like we're doing it! Thank you Jesus for the strength. Chip & I are sober. God send some of my angels over to watch over Chip. I couldn't imagine having to do this at work! Called Schauntell to say a prayer for Chip. She's depressed. I doubt if she will. I hope she does though. George called he didn't get to sleep until 3am this morning & is out working in the sun. he must be in good shape. I hope Chip comes by. I'm going to tell him he can stay here if he wants. It's closer to work, & I have AC & the company would be nice. I guess I should try to sleep. I'm starting to really not feel good. Headache. The part that I really hate is when I can't stand. But that stuff will only last a few days & thank God I have a little cash for food & stuff. I'll try to keep writing but I can't guarantee anything. Goodnight.

5:50am – I've been working on a theory about Chip, and it's just my opinion, going on what I've seen and what I know. Chip is a <u>beautiful</u> person. I've never met anyone like him before, all the people he runs with are a lot younger than him.

1:45pm – well, I just had a talk w/ Chip, brushing on the subject of all this stuff, he acted a little strange & said the reason he hangs out w/ the people that he does probably isn't the reason that I think. Instantly, I start doubting myself. (confusion) so I still like Chip (unless he's a child molester, etc) a lot. I think I'm going to just chill. All these signs & miracles has taken its toll on my dope riddled mind & body & spirit. to much info. overload. Joy wants to come over & I wouldn't mind but, I'm sure she will want to go on a spiritual mission and #1 I don't want to take from what happened yesterday. #2 what happened yesterday I doubt will ever happen again? With her anyway. So I'm going to turn that side of my brain off & get simple. try to write later... love.. (drawn happy face)

5-23-01 / 1:36 A.M.! – Not tweakin! believe it or not. I do feel very different. Don't know if there will be another entrée soon, or ever, this is the best opportunity, yet, it's not that I'm not taking it, it's just that I'm not going to stress on it. That is to say, I'm not going to look for it or anything. I'm just going to "Live", feel real good about things *that might be different tomorrow. Hopefully not, but who knows? Right now! Chip was going to take me to Leatherby's after giving Lance a ride. I passed out waiting for him. Woke up a few hours later. A little upset because Joy had called & asked me to Jack-in-the-box & grocery shopping & I kinda thought that sounded cool. But I already made plans with Chip, seems like that's always how it is w/ Joy. Right now I feel nothing but love for Joy & I want to keep it that way. I'm afraid if we spend a lot of time together, that will change, if I walk now, that's how I want to remember her. I told Chip to call if there were any problems. Assuming there would be. I would go with Joy. He didn't call until late, which I actually slept through her call so I was stuck. It's just the principal. It all worked out though. He brought me mac salad, ice cream, milk & (illegible). Ate to much. Pooped 3 times. THINK POSITIVE! Sorry, just checkin myself. While poopin. Ash called a couple of times. Weird times to call from jail. (illegible) & called Chip. Finished made the bed. Clean sheets. Invited Joy over tomorrow AM. It's cooled off. Smoked a bowl. Got Smashing Pumpkins on, having a lot of trouble seeing. Now, I'm going to pray hard & crash hard! LOVE. Bye (drawn happy face).*

6:45 – got the runs. Schauntell came by, I gave her her cross, she laughed at it, hung it on my (illegible) & forgot it. So I think I just might give it to Joy.

5/26 – 1:46pm – Been real sick! Mostly sleeping. Real sick. See ya.

5/27 – 6:26pm – A short reprieve from the agony of drying up. Chip & Lance came by. Splits a bag 3 ways, aaahh, spin then they left. I'm cleaning my house again. I don't expect any more, that's ok. Steve M called. He has diabetes now. God be with him. Last night I woke up choking on my vomit, a little freaky but I survived. Yes, that's right. I'm still alive. I will write again when I can, Love! (drawn happy face, heart, peace sign + PRAISE JESUS)

Valerie Covert

10:19pm – House clean. I'm clean. Got order signed by judge. Fully favorable. Can't make any sense out of it, also talked to Daniel today he said his dads got cancer of the colon. God Bless! Burning some insense. Mellow, I guess it's back down for me, oh well, I'm grateful for this reprieve again. I'll write when I can. Love. Bye.....M.D.C.

5/28 – 2:44am Can't sleep. Took 1 Vicodin, 1 Trazadone, 32 oz beer, many pipe hits, ate a lot). Can't quit thinking about back pay & 4 Runner. & other things. The house has the old energy about it. Candles lit, good smells. Maybe I'm just enjoying it. Far out, huh? I guess I'll give it another try, 90 meetings in 90 days. Love. Bye. Good night…(drawn quarter moon w/ smiling face). Yea, that's right! Think positive! I almost forgot, Praise Jesus!

5/28 – 9:47pm – well, let me tell you what happened today. First of all, didn't get a lot of sleep last night. Maybe because Marissa wasn't in bed w/ me. Woke up feeling good! Talked to almost everyone, ate a lot. About Sixish I made chili and it was excellent! I ate it all! Chip popped in for a minute minus Lance? Not a word was said about dope. (not that it's not on my mind) George called said he's still partying in Monterey. Talked to Teri, she didn't have a great visit w/ her mom. Chip picked me up went downtown to give Lance an ish. He was with a porn star. Went to Chips work. Got rigs & I'm home & ready for bed. Love. Goodnight. M.

5/30 – 12:11 am HB Lance (happy birthday). Can't sleep again. I hope this isn't the new schedule. I don't think it will be but I sure have enjoyed the thoughts, visions & dreams I've had! I wish I could have recorded them all! But as Teri would say, you'll remember when you need to. Not tweakin! Rum & OJ & one pipe hit o the green, kinda passed on the "D" or actually didn't pursue it. Met a nice lady. Jill. Old lady of Dennis. Had sentimental talk w/ Valerie & probably made an ASS of myself, but she knows what's up. Had a real good dream. (not sex…well…a little) Had some revelations about recovery/ sobriety, Schauntell got a dildo today. Have felt really good all day. Want Chip to feel this (doubtful). Passed on free dope & pool w/ Joy &

new friends. I kinda wish I didn't. oh well, gonna try to sleep again. MUCH LOVE!! Goodnight. MDC…

5/31 – 12:30pm FAT ISSUE! Still spinning 20 minutes later. Chip & Lance came by last night on their way out of town to score, took me to store & I contributed $10 to the cause. Chip called at 2:30am & said everything went ok, but couldn't make it by until lunch tomorrow, or later…no biggie Lance calls at 9am asks if he can kick it here till Chip shows. Chip shows up <u>on time</u>, with burgers & dope, it's all good. Yesterday, Schauntell shows up w/ Deli, we went to back quak then to Mather. Saw Cliff, Keri and a few others. Sue H. Good talk. Then to her house, naked fun w/ her new toy! (drawn happy face) Very good day! So here I am, all charged up and ready to go! Will wirte again soon! Peace, love & happiness (drawn peace sign, heart and happy face)

6/2 1:32am Yesterday Joy was the first one to call & I was ready to get out of the house, she wanted to go to Target, etc. she sounded wired so I said come & get me, a hour goes by & Schaunell calls & says she's in the hood & I told her Joy was taking me to the store, she said she could take me. I told her Joy was on her way. I think she got mad or jealous? She hung up the phone w/out saying bye? So Joy shows up about an hour later sayin she's got all her shit done & she's comin down, but she's got a big ish at home she'll split w/ me. We got to her pad. It's different. Parts clean, parts dirty, lots of signs of the kids. She's only got a little tiny bit of D left in the spoon & I'm not about to share her cotton. So she does it all in about 4 shots. My heads starting to ache real bad & she's putting a care package together. Then G(illegible) & Roger show up. (I havent' been there since she had mgr kick B & A out, haven't talked to Roger since she told them I turned her out. Immediately Roger confronts me about it. I told him the truth. I know he'll never understand, but I think he respects the fact that I was honest, it all worked out, but by this time my head's throbbin so bad I think I'm gonna puke. We get out of there fast to pay phone. Called Chip & told him what was up, he sounded very disappointed but told me he would bring some D over but I had to meet him downstairs. Head POUNDING! We did some & Joy says she's horny, something about her still really turns me on, but she says that she has to eat first, we played around for a while, it didn't work. So I'm trying to tweak on something, a while later she calls me into the room & says she's ready so we went into the bathroom to clean her up. Really cool to watch this in the mirror. Then we shaved her almost bald. A Real turn on! Back to bed for some real love making. It felt sooo good! (Real) I love Schauntell, but it's different. I guess I'll always be cursed w/ love for her, she falls asleep & I polyurethane night stand. Up all night. I hardly did any dope at all, it was making me nauseous by sun up I felt like SHIT! Need food! She finally woke up about noon, things are comfortable, we discussed her staying here for a while. She's asking me if she's my girlfriend again. I couldn't answer but I'm feeling close to being a couple again. I told her. I kdon't know about that but I have BOUNDARIES. #1 no bed hoppin & chill on the dope. (she's got a new 4 day boyfriend that Jesus himself gave her) so she just says shes going to see him, I said I thought we discussed that. She said she wasn't ready. No biggie? Worked out a little Vicodin deal. Took Julus to get them. Dropped Joy off at Denny's for her date, I'm kinda strung out, still haven't eaten. Good time w/ Julius, good times, soul music, car overheating. R cap blows in my face, burn, came home. Got cool, met Dennis. He's really cool. Talked to Chip, big deal going down here tomorrow, meet at Joy's later, he's alright (doesn't have any idea!) so here I am, not tired yet but in a good place. Been neglecting Marissa. Must stop that! Well, I think I'm going to try & crash. Peace. Love & Happiness! (drawn happy face) MDC…

9:39am – didn't sleep well at all. Yesterday I think I only did about a nickel and still at 9:30 the next day still feel kinda wired, hows that for low tolerance? I wish Joy would have left her car keys. It's still parked out there. I don't like that. Oh well, write later. Love (drawn peace sing, heart, happy face) MDC

5:35pm Joy gets taught a lesson on respect & stepping on toes (but probably didn't learn & she's on probation here) and I work on my patience. (Drawn frustrated face). I've got to do something. No food, poor Marissa's been neglected again. Heartburn is setting in again (2 Rolaids left) Jeuleus doesn't have my $36 yet, no word from Chip or

Justin (Big Surprise) I think I'm to sick to walk to 7-11. Bitch Bitch Bitch. I'm sure it'll all work out. In 2 months this will all be behind me, thank God. Chip just called & I'm expecting him to make it all better soon. I guess Justin split w/ Joys $. she should have listened to me. Oh well, she like to learn the hard way. George is supposed to show later w/ a lot of cash. See ya later (drawn happy face) M.D.C.

6/4 11:20am Last night Chip & L did come by, we got spun, went grocery shopping at Safeway. Got a lot of stuff other than food. Lots of good sales. Had wonderful eye contact w/ check out girl. Blonde hair, aqua eyes. (Beautiful!) I I I went home, George & Abble show up, they ended up going to tittie bar, I stayed home & tweaked. Joy called a few.

4:45am – Getting ready to pass out! I haven't done any dope for over a day, a little diarrhea. Talked to Joy's grandparents today. I must start being strong. I know I can! I have a lot to write but, I don't think I'm going to make it, I'm fading real fast, thinking about adopting Sammy again. (Probably just the drugs). (drawn sad face). Schauntell came over w/ Osterich burger. Maybe that's what's wrong w/ stomach! We took Marissa to Howe Park. Couldn't have been a more beautiful day. I could not believe how much attention she attracts. Lots of people staring! She got a little sketchy at the end, but we made it, I think she had fun. Must be strong & think positive. It was really cool seeing Brenda & her son & friends. I also had a really good time at auction w/ G. Must crash now. LOVE (with the happy face drawn in the O) MDC

6/6 3:13am – Yes I did crash earlier tonight. Woke up screaming calf cramps in both legs. Scared to go back to sleep. Yesterday was just another, unusual full of surprise. Stayed up ALL night, night before last, Chip called early & asked if he could drop Lance off. I thought co. would be cool, so he came by & I was still flyin from the night before. It looked like he was gonna crash. I offer him my room or an ish. He bought a huge $20, stuck a huge rock in a rig & was going to make it last until we take Mar to the vet. I guess I wasn't thinking & split it in

1/2 . he did his and definitely woke up (quick) we tweak some. Then went to Dimple, had fun! Got stars, still ampin hard, we went home chip came over w/ burgers asked Lance if he needed any Lance didn't. I did. Little worried I wouldn't get paid back, I guess Chip left a bunch w/ Lance, Chip left, we did big ones! Had a lot of fun! Just tweakin. Hard. Listening to good Loud R & R. Joy's grandparents calling non stop. (wearing me out bad, I told AM I <u>will</u> get a hold of her & I did) Ended her & Lance up for deal w/ car stereo, Chip even envoloved. He wouldn't come up though. Lance thought she's cute. Everything worked out, but I did donate the last of my D to the cause. Joy been doing Bunk D for days. She looks <u>a lot</u> worse than she did when she left here a few days ago. Herpes on chin. Must be havin a lot of sex. Depressed but she's positive that this is the decipel God hooked her up w/. Whatever? I've been hearing that a lot from her. I just remind her that I thought she's full of shit. & remember I said that, but she wont. Lance took off. She spread some Chaos around the house, used the shit out of my phone, broken up w/ new decipal boyfriend a few times, took me to store, waiting for boyfriend to pick her up. I love her. I make no secret of that, but that girl is just nuts. Hasn't called Sammy in 2 weeks. I'm having a hard time dealing w/ her & whole family. I got the house picked up & me fed. I'm very sore! & tired haven't done an ish in a long time. Don't even know where it is . look before I forget. Me & L just did Big ish. Someone starts beating on the door. Car I don't know in driveway. Not concerned aobut what we had laying out. I opened the door, there's Eduardo & new sober friend. Came by to show how good they are doing. This, I am going to give them what they expect. So when Ed was done fixing me, I just let myself be spun! They didn't stay for long at all & I imagine they will have to catch a few extra meetings after that one. & Ed whispers to me, he went by Bills & cops were there. He's preachin to me, but that there tells me he's already set up to fail. So, oh well. Back to where I was. Joy left, got the tape I made for her, she said she left something for me. It was a neat picture of Sammy Sue, yea, oh yea, I cried. I'm going to get ahold of Sammy Sue & have blind faith that my God will send me down the right path. Talking to Alice Mae, she said Sammy wants a Barbie & some GOO for her birthday. GOO, now that doesn't sound like Sammy does it? (drawn happy face). Anyway, early evening after

The Bottom is Six Feet Under

some Vicodin, food I passed out and woke up yelling Joy's name? This being linked to her would be so much easier if she would pull the dick out of her mouth & her head out of her ass! Chip called just then, & I was happy I was asleep. & said Lance was coming tomorrow. I'm cool w/ that, actually, if we didn't' answer the phone, probably would have had almost perfect day. Lance w/ his headset on telling a different girl every 10 minutes that he was busy & would call back in a while. Most of the chicks are in recovery. Really got to know him better today. We talked a lot about the 3 of us getting sober 2gether he gave me his bracelet w/ Stephanie's name on it? I gave the lizard maglite I stole from Joy & told him don't let her see it. Pat called. I told her I wanted help w/ my back pay, she talked to me like I was a child. I almost hope she knows I'm on it. & that's why she talks that way to me. But she said she would help. I don't know if I did the right thing by asking her, but she really is the only one I trust the most about this, I really just need to dry up. When I'm wired, I can't. Not spend all my money. That's the big fear. Rite Aid w/ Chip. The Bargain Bins. Anyway, I'll write again soon, this pen is getting easier to write with, Marissa to vet today & get to say hi to Katrina, might end up taking to Lance. Out of test strips & money. But a lot of love in my heart! Peace, love and happiness. M.D.C. (drawn happy face)

6/9 1:30am – To quote a song by Stained, "It's been a while". Lots of things going on and been spun for 7 days. I don't know where to begin. Schauntell quit taking her meds, gonna try GV miracle water. So far, not working at all. I've seen a side of her that was just too much like Joy.

Running out of time. Running out of space.

6/12 3:30pm – Sorry I havent' written, I'll bet you thought I was sober & sleeping, no, spun & tweakin so bad I couldn't write.

6/13 2:15pm – Cant get it together long enough to tell you what's been going on, not much actually. No dope today so far. Spun hard! Until today. Since 12 days ago. If I'm forced to dry up now it's going to be a tough road to hoe! Haven't spoken to my God lately. I did make a few crosses, had fun playing w/ Lance. Today he's grounded on the couch. Last night to Chips for steak, wine & issues that's about all I can write now. Try later if im not in dt's. bye. MC

6/17 2:35am – Hi. Remember me? Well, same shit, not much change. Thumbs are cut up & sore, passin out on the john. I'll write tomorrow. Bye. MC

6/18 10:20am – Our target date. Again. Yesterday was fathers day. Came down all day. Very depressing. Jess called! Teri brought new candle. Karrie shows up out of the blue. Dave's been cheatin on her w/ skanky chicks. She just happens to have some dope. We had a good talk. Val called. We all talked (Note from Author: When I called him that day, I had NO idea what kind of shape he was in). Chip & Lance come & drop off some dope, can't seem to get high. Crashed late. Lance comes over they quit at 12. Later MC

5:40pm – I had my come down list & was going through it fast, got a little side tracked & ended up getting the MG running! Can you believe that? Juleus came over & gave me $40? Chip came to pick up Lance & passed out on couch. Lance & I jonsin bad! Bye. MC (drawn happy face)

June 26 7:40pm – WOW (drawn face w/ very wide eyes) CHAOS, AT LAST! I'd forgotten how miserable it is. Sober since Father's Day. Not totally by choice, but Chip & Lance were so this time I had to follow it, it was going fair, no food, no money but sober, smiling. (Glowing faces). People noticed the difference in me. But, it was only a matter of time before I folded like a cheap deck of cards. And I did. Sunday I called to see how Karrie & turtle were doing (and to check out the dope situation, why lie?) She sounded sketchy & said she would call me back. She did as I was climbing into bed at 11pm. Said she had some D & she'd be over. Got drunk on Rum waiting for her. She called again at 1am. Then at 9am. Monday, finally showed up at 11am, Lance crashed on the couch. (moral dilemma #1) Karrie *and a ton of bunk D. I immediately do a VERY large dose of type B & felt it. If it was Chips I would have been doin the FISH (drawn fish) for an hour or more, but I did feel it. Moral dilemma #2. I told Chip I wouldn't do any unless it was with them, anyway, Lance & Joy just showed up w/ chew, candy & new weapon. They look nice & charged up. From then on, the chaos starts building faster w/ Chip & typical Joy chaos. It finally gets so bad I had to throw them out. Joy didn't mind. She was ready to sink her fangs into Lance. It didn't take long for me to get the good energy back in my sanctuary. Then call the Chip I never saw & demand him to bring a fat issue. He did w/ Brian we spun hard. Went to Walgreens at 3am & looked at everything they had.*

6/27 7:25am – I apologize for rarely finishing an entry anymore. Life has become very unstable & unpredictable lately, but I'm sure that will change along with my lifestyle.

7/1 3:20am – I'm going to catch up on all the events lately.

7/2 5:05am – slept for a while last pm. Little Lances' B-day party. Chuck E Cheeses. Got him camera & shades, saw Stacey. Going back where I left off. The next day was Ozz fest, which we, the three musketeers, were supposed to go to. Sober. Talked to Lance & Joy a few times throughout the night. Sketchy. I'm sure they had sex, but I wanted to go to concert. Chip said it was off, Lance said it's on. By am Chip feeling VERY guilty! I feel sick. I was going to take Karrie's car to the shop at 9 & Lance said we have to leave at 9. I couldn't get a hold of her anyway. I decided to stay & hang w/ Chip & meet Justin. Lance & his buddy, leather jacket obsessed w/ my guitar show up spun. We call Chip demand he comes. None of us can think straight. 3 hours later we finally come up w/ a plan where we score some dope at the concert & me & chip take Karrie's car. We get to Karrie's house & chill for a few, just the three of us. Everything's cool. Except Lance shows up w/ uninvited guest, that's right, Joy. Instantly we drop out. Chip hates her. Course Lance & I'm having problems w/ it. They swear nothing happened & Joy even puts on a real good act about Lance sitting too close to her. She begs me to just hang w/ her & karrie. I agree, knowing it would fuck up all other plans. So Karrie's trippin on Lance. We all talk Joy playin her councelor act & as usual creating Chaos. Kinda settle it. Joy goes to say bye to Lance. I walk outside & there she is, legs wrapped around Lance hugging him. I'm really tired of playing the fool. She comes back, calls John & wants to fix Karrie up. 5150? She ends up leaving w/ him. Ok by me. Poor Karrie isn't used to this kind of shit. Me & chip leave he said we had to go a couple of places Karrie might not be comfortable. So we'll meet her in a bit at my pad, me… never questioning Chip end up at adult book store. I forgot to mention at Walgreens chip got a pump like mine & had an idea about modifying it, we spent a while in the store, tripping, then went to my house. Leave it to Chip. Justin & Ros & animals waiting for us at 8am. Oops. Got a little side tracked. I'll pick it up later, got a lot of shit to today & it's going to be 102 out today. (drawn happy face) M.D.C.

7/5 1:15am – Still flakey, sober except for green! Down stairs neighbor & new friend, Steve. Joy's here. Saw Roger. Crazy shit.

7/10 6:20am – Yeah, here I am. I seen to have gotten lost somewhere, I'm not going to give up. I have been avoiding reality a lot lately. Hoping God will take care of everything. Well, I have to do the footwork, but I don't know if I can? I'm so funckin overwhelmed, I can't think. It's too late. I can't pull it off, unless I get some back pay. (drawn light bulb) (guess he had an idea) call Bruce or Jim & ask if I will receive any back pay. At least I'll know if I have to trip & can't let myself get out there. Don't loose track of time! GET ENERGY – HARMONY!! HEY! WAKE UP!! I have been praying for strength all night & I only get bits & pieces. & it seems I'm alone. And a fat issue last pm didn't make your head any clearer. Or all the green bud. Well, time is running short on this journey. If I give up, it'll really fuck w/ Jesy. For right now, all I can say is, give me strength, in Jesus name! I'm not really as sick and twisted as this journal may portray me. Think positive! (drawn happy face)

The Bottom is Six Feet Under

Aug 4, 2001 Jessica's on a plane now & they're telling me she wont be escorted to United in LA. Back pay almost spent, almost killed terilee the other day. MG's looking good & insured. Teri's been calling my friends, etc & telling them I'm an unfit father to Jess & marissa, Sue actually is talking about taking marissa from me. I'm tweaking. I just want to get my princess in my arms!

NOTE FROM AUTHOR:

THIS WAS THE LAST ENTRY IN THIS JOURNAL. THE NEXT ONE IS DATED STARTING IN OCTOBER. THERE IS NO MONTH OF SEPTEMBER.

DURING THE MONTH OF SEPTEMBER OF THAT YEAR, I FLEW JESSICA OUT TO SEE HER DAD. SHE WAS 8 YEARS OLD.

ON THIS VISIT, HE TOOK HER OUT FOR ICE CREAM. HE SKIPPED THE SUGAR FREE FOR HIMSELF. SUBSEQUENTLY, HE SLIPPED INTO A COMA IN THE NIGHT AND OUR 8 YEAR OLD DAUGHTER CALLED ME (2500 MILES AWAY) SCREAMING AND CRYING THAT SHE COULDN'T GET HER DADDY TO WAKE UP – I TOLD HER TO HANG UP AND CALL 911, TELL THEM JUST WHAT SHE TOLD ME, AND THEN TO CALL ME BACK. THEY RUSHED HIM TO THE HOSPITAL WITH A BLOOD SUGAR OF OVER 800. HE WAS REALLY FREAKED OUT WHEN THEY CALLED ME FROM THE HOSPITAL…HE KNEW I WOULD BE UPSET BECAUSE HE HAD CONSCIOUSLY MADE THE DECISION TO EAT ICE CREAM WITH SUGAR – WHEN HE WAS RELEASED FROM THE HOSPITAL, I TOLD HIM THAT I COULD NO LONGER LET HIM VISIT JESSICA UNSUPERVISED. I KNOW THAT THAT REALLY HURT HIM, BUT I EXPLAINED TO HIM THAT IF HE CANNOT EVEN TAKE CARE OF HIMSELF, HOW CAN I TRUST THAT HE CAN TAKE CARE OF OUR CHILD. IT WAS VERY DAMAGING TO JESS TO BE IN THAT SITUATION. SHE WAS TERRIFIED.

THAT WAS THE LAST TIME JESS GOT TO PHYSICALLY SEE HER DAD. ONE OF HER CHRISTMAS GIFTS FOR 2002 WAS THAT WE BOUGHT HER DAD A TICKET TO COME OUT

TO HAWAII TO SEE US IN FEBRUARY, UNFORTUNATELY, HE DIDN'T MAKE IT IN TIME.

10/26/02 – 1:33am / 12:33 Daylight savings time. Back checks at Walgreens w/ Joe & JD for costume for Mikey & rigs for Chip. Back at Brea's. Sick. Nikki shows up, surprise bible study. I really like her attitude. Thanx. Write you later. (drawn happy face).

10/27 8:09 am Brea, Nikki & I on recon mission at Spams hotel. Recovered Brea's grams, silver chain & misc. other items. Forgive us Father! Must focus on finding a residence. See ya.

10/28 4 pm – Chilled at Ruth's all day. Saw Tom B. Sr & talked w/ Tom Jr. didn't accomplish much, oh well, Nikki's <u>still to Brea's</u> playin Hustler, called Robert's parents. No word yet, he should be out any time. I miss the hell out of Mike too he should be out soon. Getting the run around from Rick, he's about to make my gank list. Got a threatening call from Pam. She must not know threats make me angry! Please forgive my sins Father. Thank you! (drawn happy face)

Halloween – Very bad mood! Been in pain all day! Me & Nik at Ruth's tonight. We'll see what happens? Got a few things done today. Going to think more & talk to you later. (drawn happy face)

11/11/02 1:40pm – Jamba Juice w/ Joe & Brian. What a typically BIZARRE day & chain of events. Going to try to get straight. Back to right.

11/? 2:30am – Laying on bathroom floor. Room 209. Best Buy Motel. Brea & Robert & Robert resting comfortably, me however… (illegible) today!

11/15/02 – far out more strange days. Just like old times too many bizarre things to write. Robert & I looked at a 4 plex off of Auburn

Blvd. Fireplace, balcony, garage. I like it! Met Chip downtown. Traded a box of rigs for a bag of shit! Went to Brea's.

 11/17 4am – Have not been able to make an entree due to severe illness, puking for hours. haven't been able to eat <u>anything</u> for days. Stayed at Lisa's last night. Slept like a rock. I guess Brea stole something out of Lisa's daughter's room. Robert caught her so we traded the ring she gave him for dope. Not a whole lot has happened in the last few days. Lisa might let me stay here. Robert started dragon tattoo. I'll probably end up in the hospital if I don't get a lot better soon. Very dihderated & dizzy. tried to get ahold of Jess unsuccessfully, will try again tomorrow. (drawn frustrated face)

 Thanksgiving Day 2002, Flat on my back for 10 days at Roberts parents house. Lost 43 pounds in 2 weeks. Dad & Robert took me to Dr.'s appt where I passed out while the nurse weighed me. Went to hospital. Got rehydrated & released. Still no solid food. Two days pass.

 11/27 am – I wake up feeling 25% better. Meet Grandma & Vickie & Dee Dee. What a wonderful family! I'm blessed to just know these people. Thank you Jesus! Signing off for now. In Jesus' name, let me feel better tomorrow. (drawn happy face)

 11/30 11:15am – Bad night! Passed out Bad! A couple of x's, once woke up w/ my TV on top of me. feels like I broke my arm, that's ok I fight back! I just hope mom & dad don't get freaked out. Might go horse back riding at Joes? Thank you Jesus, for this day. (drawn happy face) later….

 12/1 – Sunday 11:45 passed out. Mon.

 12/2 – yesterday was not a very good day. God, please let this be a better one. In Jesus name! thank you. (drawn happy face)

Valerie Covert

4:10pm – another day shot to hell! Nikki called, said she's doing well, wants to meet & give me some money? had a big list of stuff to do went to leave no gas. Asked mom & dad for a couple of $ they didn't have a dime. So I'm waiting for Robert & family to get here & drop off his car & give me some gas $ to take them back to Breas.

12/5 3:45am – not a good day at all! In Jesus name, please let me get better! Bye.

12/15/02 9:30pm – Been home for two days, health improved a little, up all night puking. Not fun. aches & pains all day. Started to eat a little. Things sure would be <u>a lot</u> tougher w/out mom & dad. They really are the salt of the earth! Don't know whats up w/ Robert? I'm worried about him. everybody is. Been talking w/ Nikki, can't afford that! Val says they're going to fly me out there next month. Won't get my hopes or Jess' up. I'll still pray for it! have to go to Dr.'s tomorrow. hope & pray it helps! & get my hat! anyway, gonna go chill for a few. I'll write again soon. Thank you Jesus! (drawn happy face)

It's me again. I sure hope I'm not getting on the Thompsons nerves, cause it's sure comfy here. Bye. (drawn happy face).

<u>VERY</u> stormy tonight! Jesus, watch over all your children. Saw Rick today for 1st x in a long x. it's usually really good to see him. he's got some kinda poison gas in his house, he looked unhealthy, as if I do? anyway, I just need to stay focused & positive and things will start to fall into place. Thanks J! (drawn happy face) See ya!

12/16 am – Spent most of yesterday w/ Nikki. had an allright day by that p.m. we were getting at each others throats. Nothing ventured, nothing gained. Bought myself a DVD player yesterday. Buyers remorse. Oh well.

12/18 am – Managed to keep most of a cup of noodles down. Thank you J! & going to try to get some Ensure & see Dr.'s & do about a million other things today. Who knows talk to ya later. (drawn happy face)

12/19/02 2:25pm – Must make this quick! Well, yet another twist to the saga! Robert shows up all spun (who isn't) & says I have to move out. Just what I need. PG & E saw I was staying here & they'll fuck w/ his disability so on the road again! But I got the most Beautiful pics of Jess!!! (drawn happy face). today and some clothes from Mom! What I was really excited about was the box they came in! Perfect packing box! Later. thank you J. (drawn happy face)

(drawn happy face) High, packed all day. Could tell Dad was in a hurry to get me out. Robert & Brea didn't show until 8 or 9 pm! Not am. Everything worked out. I'm not trippin. I got a package from mom & Valerie! (drawn happy face) new school pics from Jess. Beautiful pics! nice clothes by this pm. I could barely move. Rob had to load the car, but I managed to eat a little stew. Robert & Brea went to Walgreens, I'm sittin in her room, by myself, I know Robert's trippin on thiefs. But me? oh well. Talk to ya laer, it seems' that I talk to you more than anybody else. I used somebody elses credit card to pay my phone bill, I'm sorry! In Jesus name, please forgive me? Love (drawn happy face)

12/23/02 4:55 A.M. – Sorry I haven't checked in. (drawn sad face) still drifting, on my quest for Chaos & trauma. Stayed at Rick & Robertas they are a carbon copy of me & Nikki. More than a little Chaos there, it's too bad, they don't know how good they got it. (DOPE) anyway, I've been eating more & more. I looked at my body naked – CORPES! About 135 lbs. working on it! got all my stuff from Robert's parents. Alot of it R & R's gonna try & get it in storage today! & find an apartment and about a trillion other things. In J's name, please help me do these things! Talk to you later. My cornbeef surprise patties are wantin out! Love you! (drawn happy face).

Hi there. Christmas Eve Day. *3:00pm* – Hasn't been too bad, talked to Mom, visited Ruth, Don & Becky had another mammoth son, named him Alex. that's ok. having a baby named after you is to much responsibility. So now it's time to call Jess. I'm very tired! I was finally able to finish my Corned beef surprise, I'll try to get back 2 u soon, but? thank you Jesus. Me. (drawn happy face)

12/27/02 3:30 A.M. – Hi, yep, you guessed it. been sober for a few, Christmas called Mom & Jess & went to Ruths for ham. witch I couldn't eat, yesterday, Nikki came by for some snuggling. R & R made her leave. Robert ripped Chip off for $100. I picked up Broski & we drove around for a while. not much else to report. Gonna look for apartment.

12/28 7:30am – Aches & pains. Chest pain, heartburn & spitting up blood, real tired of this BS but, I aint givin up!!! I made some kick ass hamburger helper last pm. Rick & Roberta didn't like it. Rick said it made him deathly ill. Got a lot to do today. I'll write later. thank you Jesus. LOVE (drawn happy face)

1/4/03 – Move out day & I'm WORTHLESS. Kristi gave me this pen for my journal & I just wanted to give it a test drive. I like it alot. It's beautiful outside! But I must go fetch a pizza. I'll write more later. thank you J. (drawn happy face)

1/4/03 Well I guess this will be the last day at R & R's appt. they busted their butts & got everything moved out, I got a deeper deep dish couldn't eat. Didn't make it to my surgery yesterday, but, I went to Nate & Amy's. Nate had to walk me home saw Buck on the way almost passed out. Buck had to hold me up. I don't think I'm being punished but...

1/9 11:00 A.M. – Hi. Well one more time been flat on my back for a week, (pneumonia) but thank God for J & Lisa! I made a quick get away from R & R;s over here then got extremely sick although I've been eating better! I belive I need to explore assisted living.

The Bottom is Six Feet Under

1/10 2:56pm – haven't answered the phone in days. quality of life diminishing rapidly. Constant state of misery. Combine that with loneliness, resentment, anger, fear & confusion, etc. I don't know where to turn to! I pray & I pray and I guess that's what keeps me going. Most of my friends have showed their dis loyalties. Nate threatening me. Chip burning me. even Jana thinks I took a ring from her? I know things will look better when I recover from this pneumonia, but now I just want to die! Peace, love & happiness (drawn frustrated face)

1/13 9:30 A.M. – Been up all night, Bodies extremely sore, But, it's a beautiful day! Sun is shining! I've got a ton of shit to do today. Gonna do my best to get it all done, whish me luck! Love. (drawn happy face)

1/21/03 1:50 A.M. – It's going to be rough getting caught up as usual. Never a dull moment! Been at Lisas for a few weeks now mostly on my Death bed. didn't answer the phone stayed in bed. Unfortunately, I must cut this short. I will try to get caught up soon. (drawn peace sign, heart & happy face)

1/22/03 11 P.M. – I really wonder if I'm a Chaos magnet, if somehow it follows me around or visa-versa. Trauma at Lisas! did I mention Robert's in jail. not for long. Lisa dumped Jay & didn't bother telling Jay. Now she's with Mark. Randy just got out of prison & wants to hook up w/ her. My new friend Dave really is obsessed w/ Christi.

1/22 6:00 A.M. – Sorry about all the interruptions it seems the more I make my little room my sanctuary the world outside gets more crazy. Drive by shooting 3 houses up from Lisas. Mark finally made it back? I'm very tired now. I'll write later. thanks. (drawn frustrated face)

1/22 2 P.M. – I'm tryin like Hell to catch up! Got a new friend, Dave. he's pretty cool. I think. & I'm trying to get this pen going. But,

Valerie Covert

back to Dave. So far he's given me a <u>really</u> nice 1600 watt amp & set of woofers, I just need to get my car running. I wonder if this will be a trauma free day? Anyway, I'll try & write later. I'm sure I'll have some bizarre & strange tale to tell. Peace, love & happiness. (drawn happy face)

THIS WAS THE LAST ENTRY. MATTHEW WAS FOUND DEAD IN HIS ROOM ON 1/29/03. THE OFFICIAL CAUSE OF DEATH ON THE DEATH CERTIFICATE IS DIABETIC KETOACIDOSIS. WE ALL KNOW WHAT LEAD TO IT, REGARDLESS OF WHAT FINALLY TOOK HIM.

It seems that he walked into the room and fell into a diabetic / dope coma, sliding down the door and he passed away.

Do you remember the movie City Slickers with Billy Crystal. Well, Matt and I being the movie buffs that we were had seen that movie many times. His favorite part (and the one that he could emulate to perfection) was the voice of Billy Crystal when he was talking to the calf and he said "HELLOOOOOO" He would try and call every night but for the most part it was at least every two-three days. I would answer and he would say "HELLOOOOOO". We would talk for a time and then he would talk to Jess. When he hadn't called in a couple of days, I tried to call him. His roommate at the time said that he was asleep. This was a Monday. I tried again on Tuesday and she told me he was upstairs asleep. I asked her to please let him know that Val and Jess were trying to reach him. I honestly thought he was on a binge and too ashamed to call.

On Wednesday morning I got the phone call that changed our lives forever. It was that call from his brother. He wanted to tell me early enough so that I would have myself together to tell Jessica. I still remember every word of that phone call.

Matthew's funeral was held on February10[th] 2003. There were beautiful cards handed out to the guests with a picture of a white dove in flight over the serenity prayer on one side and his obituary on the other. Jessica and I did not attend the service. She didn't want to go. It was entirely too painful. My mom went for us. She said that it was a nice service, but it was one of the saddest she had ever attended. She said there were pictures of Matt, myself and Jessica the day that we brought her home from the hospital.

Matt's obituary read:
COVERT, MATTHEW DAVID

36, loving father, son and brother, passed away on January 29th, 2003. Matt's journey through life was not always an easy one, but his good humor and genuine spirit never wavered, and will be remembered fondly by all who knew him. Survived by his daughter Jessica Autumn Covert; mother and stepfather Shirley and Lanne Seifert; brother and his wife Jeffrey and Kristi Covert, and their children Nelson and Gracie; stepmother Patricia Covert; Grandmother Jan Simmons; and numerous relatives and friends. The family would also like to thank his former wife, Valerie Covert, for being a trusted friend to him throughout his life. Matt was preceded in death by his father Richard Covert, and grandparents James and Gladys Covert. In lieu of flowers, the family requests gifts be made to the American Diabetes Association. Private Services will be held on Monday, February 10th.

The tributes in his local paper were:

I am filled with sorrow to learn of Matthew's death. My family and I were neighbors of the Coverts on Warrego Way for many years, and I watched him grow up. Matt played with and went to school with my children. Shirley was a very good friend of mine, and I am sad that I have lost touch with her. The last time I saw her was shortly after my wedding nearly 11 years ago. Shirley, if you are reading this, I'd love to see you again and give you a hug. I lost my husband Don this past summer, and I know the pain you are feeling now. Please call me at xxx-xxxx or send me an e-mail message at the address above.

Best Wishes Always,
Name obsoleted for privacy

Valerie Covert

Matt's daughter and I would like to thank all of whom have extended their sympathies, prayers and kind words. We will miss Matt every day but I am lucky enough to have 20 year (Jess 10 years) of wonderful memories of a loving and caring man who loved us deeply and with all his heart as he did all of his family and friends. He now is truly our angel.

Valerie and Jessica Covert

Matt (MACK) was not only my best friend but the older brother I never had. I cherish our friendship and will never forget him. We had such an awesome time in our teenage years together. Some of the best times were spent with him in his Datsun PU with Echo and The Bunnymen blaring. I know you are with your Dad fishing somewhere. Until we meet again my friend, sleep well and Rest in Peace.

Name obsoleted for privacy

THIS ONE ALMOST KILLED ME. THIS ONE IS FROM CHIP.

Although our friendship only spanned the last couple of years, I will always remember Matt as a trusting and caring friend who was determined to experience life to the fullest. I will never forget our many shipping excursions to Fry's Electronics, Costco and Target. Nor will I forget Matt's love for MG's, Harley's, his music, his Iguana, and most of all, his daughter. Matt's accepted the cards that life dealt him (LIFE... OR YOU CHIP), never complained, and did his best with what he had. I will sadly miss Matt, but I am grateful to have known him and honored to have been able to call him my friend.

We will always remember Matthew as the boy at the ranch. He was joy to have visit. Our sympathies to his family for your loss.

Name obsoleted for privacy

Matt had said that "some things lie so deep within us that they can't ever be taken away." That is how he saw his beautiful daughter. I can only stand here and know that flights of angles will sing him to his rest. Warmest wishes.

Name obsoleted for privacy

About 2 weeks after his death, I had a dream that the phone was ringing. It was all black around me and when I answered, I heard his voice say "HHEEELLLOOOO" just like he used to, in my dream, I said to him, "Matt, how can you be calling, I just buried you?" and all of the sudden his head started to float towards my face and he had the most brilliant smile that I have ever seen and he said to me, "I'm RIGHT here…". That dream brought me so much peace. Matt and I had always promised each other that if one of us went before the other and there were any way possible to let the other one know we were watching over the other, we would. I believe that was his way of showing me.

The most important thing that I have left of Matt, besides my memories, are his journals. That's what we have left. I still think about Matt, but only on Mondays, Tuesdays, Wednesdays, Thursdays, Fridays, Saturdays and Sundays.

Today, as I write this, in October 2007 I have one more chilling example of how far reaching something like this can be. Our daughter came to me last week and told me that she is not happy. Not just unhappy, but REALLY miserable and not wanting to live. She said that she thinks about killing herself EVERY day. This is after the 2 suicide attempts. She was very serious and crying out for help. You can't imagine the thoughts that raced through my head. We talked for a long time and she revealed to me that she is depressed and thinks that she may need medication. I immediately called the local hospital's psychiatric ward and told them what she said. They gave me the steps to take next and I spoke with her and explained that in order for her to get medication, she would have to be admitted into the adolescent psychiatric ward at the hospital and be "evaluated". She understood, and was in so much pain, was willing to do whatever it took to feel better. Thank God that she came to me.

We went immediately down to the emergency room and told them that she was feeling suicidal. They admitted her. It was the second most painful thing that I have ever had to do…the first being telling her about her daddy dying and then leaving her there that day. I knew that it is for

Valerie Covert

the best. She was escorted by 2 armed guards to the unit where we had to say goodbye. I left there in complete shock and was numb. I was also relieved that she was in a place where they knew how to help to her (to some extent). As painful as is was for me to leave her there…the alternative was unthinkable.

The next afternoon, she was "evaluated" by the psychiatrist and he called me after meeting with her. He told me that his diagnosis is that she suffers from depression and Post Traumatic Stress Disorder. He said that one of the first things that she said to him was that she had never dealt with her dad's death and then she cried and cried.

Here we are, 6 years later and we're still dealing with the effects of Matt's problem. She is now actively in therapy and she and I are taking a trip out to California so that we can visit his grave. I will give her time to sit there and talk to him…yell at him….cry…whatever she needs to do to say goodbye. Every year on the anniversary of his death I go and get a flower lei and find a secluded spot at the beach and talk to him and throw the flowers to the ocean in memory of him.

It's now 2008 and we have returned from our trip to visit Matt's grave. I think that it helped Jess a little. She doesn't' believe that he is there. He is with her. And I think she's right. Still, it was good.

With her permission, Jessica has let me share with you the note that she left at her dad's grave. It reads:

I am expected to cry because you are here. I will not. Because you are not here. You cannot be contained by a slab of cement put here by someone who only knew your name. Your life cannot be put into date because it's never ending. You are the cold on my cheeks. You are the air I breathe. You are my regret and you are my childhood. To say I miss you is a dramatic understatement. My feelings could never be written. I will not cry because there is nothing here that reminds me of you. You were not a blank slab of concrete blending in with the rest. You were not these bright flowers I leave. You were not my father, you were much more. You were my God, my best friend and my confidant. I will not say "rest in peace". You are not resting. You are awake while others are sleeping. I know I don't cry, but Daddy, I never stop thinking about you. I love you more than anything, <u>forever</u>.

Inst.
Love, Jessica

The Bottom is Six Feet Under

    Well, we have made it to 2009. Jessica, I am ecstatic to say that she is feeling much better, is no longer medicated and has finished High School early and has her very first job. It has been a long road for us. It has been a long road for all of Matt's family and friends too.

    It is now January 29, 2010, the 7th anniversary of his death. I am finally finishing this story. Although we still hurt and we still struggle, Jess and I are two strong women. We will survive this and more. Will you?

Here are 2 actual pages from his journals.

Valerie Covert

to be seen. Imagine, up all night again, good dope, did a few cool things, hooked up the waterfall (for serenity.) finally filled out Jess' card, hope there's enough postage on it. Kinda tired now. Starting to get heartburn. No Rolaids. Shit! feeling extremely mellow, sitting on that damn stool all night just doesn't work, my back is killing me. Should take a Vicodin & I got a ton of em. Kinda a trip lookin at pictures last night some of them I looked way sucked up! tore up! but Jess looks great in all of them. That's about it for now, bye. Love ✝☮☺✌... ☀ Jesus is my savior. B.G. 154 15"4 7:26 p.m. Zapped by the heat, finally called Chip & told him Marissa & I would be down in the sun, too & Sue called & said she would be right over w/ meds. ETC. & to have Juleus w/ me, so I put the leash on Marissa & went down, sat in sun for awhile, Mar. went into front yard of neighbors, the gang of young Mexican kids came over crowding Mar. She seemed fine though, "alot better than me." So she poops on the lawn, then starts eating grass, then weeds, then anything she can get in her mouth. Well we got our 15+ min- in the sun; & I can't hang. I go to pick her up & she flips out trying to get away. does a death roll w/ leash on. I hold her up high branch style, she even looks like she's going to bite me, she jumps out of my hand, lands on concrete. I don't think it hurt her but I think it woke her up. So I think she just got spooked. We'll just have to take it slow. Just now starting to feel better myself. Chip & I went to 7-11, on the way to the car, Mexicans working on cars probably the chiva connect. Black people carport opposite us either crack or weed, & I this place, last year was like a senior complex, quiet & clean, now there's grafitti on the street, Chip said, there's the chiva, there's the crack, & here's the crank all in separate sides of the court. I

The Bottom is Six Feet Under

Stayed at Rick & Roberta's they are a carbon copy of me & Nikki more than a little chance there, it's too bad, they don't know how good they got it. (OOPS) anyway I've been eating more & more I looked at my body naked CORPSE! I'm about 135 LBS.! Working on it! got all my stuff from Roberta's parents, alot of it a R&R's gonna try & get it in storage today! & find an apartment and about a trillion other things. In J's name please help me do these things! Talk to you later My Corned beef Suprise patties are Wantin' out! Love you! ☺ Hi there Christmas Eve Day, 3:00 P.M. Hasn't been too bad, talked to Mom, Visited Ruth, Ron & Becky had another mammoth son, named him Alex, that's o.k. having a baby named after you is too much responsibility. So now its time to call Jess. I'm Very tired. I was finally able to finish My Corned Beef-Suprise. I'll try to get back 2 U soon but thank you Jesus, Me ☺ 12-27-02 3:30 A.M. Hi, yep you guessed it been Sober for a few. Christmas called Mom & Jess & went to Ruth's for 1 a.m. Wish I could've eat, yesterday Nikki came by for some snuggling R&R Made her leave Robert Ripped chip off for $100. & picked up Bobbi (Shawn) & we drove around for awhile. Not much else to report. gonna look for apartment

91

Made in the USA
San Bernardino, CA
25 August 2018